Marked by Miracles

Journey with the Divine

Chaplain Dixey R. Behnken

(Lieutenant Colonel-Retired) U.S. Army

Marked by Miracles
Journey with the Divine

All the stories in this book are true. Some names and identifying details have been changed to protect the identity of the people involved.

Order additional copies of this book from Amazon.com

Cover Designer: Christine Roszak

ISBN: 978-1-64836-065-7 (Hardback)

ISBN: 978-1-64836-066-4 (Paperback)

ISBN: 978-1-64836-067-1 (ebook)

dixeybehnkenbooks@gmail.com

PLEASE VISIT MY WEBSITE:

www.markedbymiracles.com

First Printing 2022

Printed in United States of America

Appreciation for
MARKED BY MIRACLES

I found an allure about Marked by Miracles, particularly because Dixey is so real in telling the stories that contain wisdom and life beneath their lines. Each entry is laced with both subtle and transparent lessons from a man's journey with God, and God with the man. Dixey's compilation of experiences will help you recognize the purposeful ways and wondrous works of the Faithful One, who weaves together a life message from threads of grit and grace. A must read for anyone exploring their own faith or considering Christian ministry. -***Rear Admiral Brent W. Scott,*** **Chief of Chaplains, U.S. Navy**

Your book is remarkable! Some readers will not be able to cease reading!
-***Donald Stephens,*** **Founder and Director of Mercy Ships**

I found Dixey's book thoughtful, uplifting and inspiring. It reminded me that even though you face challenges in life, God comes through. Chaplain Behnken served as my 82nd Airborne 307th Engineer Battalion Chaplain where he inspired Soldiers and life for the unit and our families. Later as the Commanding General of Fort Leonard Wood, MO, Dixey and I served together again. He was our Family Life Chaplain and the Brigade Chaplain for the 1st Training Brigade. He had a positive impact on the entire command. Dixey's book will help the reader discover ways to find God in the highs and lows of life. -***Robert B Flowers, Lieutenant General (Retired),*** **U.S. Army Former Commanding General, Army Corps of Engineers**

I have really enjoyed these exciting stories. I first met Dixey 40 years ago at Asbury Seminary. His noteworthy dependence on God's direction is so inspirational. -***Rev. Dr. James W. Taylor Jr. (Skip),*** **Minister of Word and Sacrament of the Evangelical Presbyterian Church, National Instructor for the Walk Thru the Bible (WTB) and Field Training Staff for International Christian Ministries (ICM)**

This is an amazing read about the miracles God has provided. The author, Dixey, is a true man of God who has continued to practice what he believes and preaches.-***Dr. Klon Kitchen, Jr.*** **Ecclesiastical Endorser, Chaplaincy Full Gospel Churches**

Dixey's unwavering and tenacious faith led him into some very interesting situations! His wit, candor and deep insights will make you laugh and at the same time challenge you to greater depths of faith. ***-Janet Benge,* author of 50 books, Christian Heroes: Then and Now Series; and 25 books, American Heroes Series, YWAM Publishing**

There are so many incredible stories God has told through your life. I pray this book will encourage many people through your encounters of faith and trusting God around the world. -***Paul H. Boge,* author of *Father to the Fatherless,* and *Hope for the Hopeless.* Speaker, Filmmaker, Producer and Professional Engineer**

A real page-turner. We need a book like this to show us God is still working and speaking to us today. Personally, I felt part of many stories. Each chapter spoke to me. This book blew me away. At the end, I wanted more. -***Dwight Coleman,* Lifetime Friend, Program Construction Manager and Consultant**

Your book is a great read! You write with wisdom and a good mix of the reality of daily living and seeking God for more miracles. The stories of healing and deliverances are so authentic and moving; they've inspired me deeply. -***Keith Warrington,* Director, Youth with A Mission, Berlin, Germany**

Your book is wonderful! I find it hard to stop reading. It is interesting, well-written and sometimes down-right inspiring!!! -***Marion Warrington,* Co-Leader with husband, Keith; Jugend Mit Einer Mission (JMEM)-Berlin, Worship Leader; Songbooks: Teach Us Lord; The Good Land; Close to You**

What a great collection of stories from decades up until recently! And all of them true. You are a great writer, and I found myself fascinated to see what was going to happen next! I love how you have navigated so many various seasons of life, but always up for an adventure. ***-Jim Orred,* Mentoring International Staff of Youth with a Mission, Ambassador-at-large**

Dixey's book is worth the read! This memoir of cascading encounters with the power of God chronicle how God was more than able to do the astonishing. He was as surprised by each event as we are! I commend this book to all who want to find their faith encouraged by the lively, dynamic fresh surprises shared in an easy-to-read manner. Each event was lived out through the life of an Army chaplain, spared from death or trouble, by the power of God again and again. ***-Rev. David Chòtka*** **(B.A.M. Div. Th.M. D. Min.) Director of Spirit-Equip Ministries; Chair, Alliance Pray! Team (C&MA Canada); author and International Conference Speaker**

This is an exciting and challenging read. The author is honest in confessing his anger with God for his stroke, and the fear that a second one may take his life. Readers will delight in so many well-told stories, but more will thrill at his faith, and be challenged to believe more deeply. -***Maxie Dunnam,*** **served 14 years as the fifth President of Asbury Theological Seminary; pastored 5,000-member Christ United Methodist Church in Memphis, Tennessee for 12 years; Dunnam is author of 40 books.**

Dedicated to:

My loving wife, Julianne (Kiracofe) Behnken; my greatest encourager, life inspiration and love of my life who has accompanied me through most of these life events. Her faith is courageous; her love contagious, and her hope unbounded.

~and to~

Our Children: Rachael Erin, Lukas Frederick, Hope Rayanne, Brandon David

and Grandchildren

Table of Contents

Foreword

The writer of Hebrews 11 records that "The fundamental fact of existence is that this trust in God, this faith, is the firm foundation under everything that makes life worth living. It's our handle on what we can't see. The act of faith is what distinguished our ancestors; it set them above the crowd" (The Message). That could be said of Dixey and Julie as well. Like our ancestors in Hebrews, they are a *people of unusual obedience,* a critical factor in the lives of those who choose to believe God for the miraculous. The historical record of this book affirms that principle.

I have observed over decades with Dixey, that discovering aspects of the character and nature of God has produced a *practical theology* applied to the realities of life, from marital conflicts, finances and felons to healing and living with the effects of a stroke. He has modeled that what we call "miracles" are evidence of man's trust and agreement with a God whose perspective is not bound by human limitations.

It is not surprising that the latest chapter in Dixey and Julie's lives is *focused on the abandoned child.* It was there in the beginning with their first commitment to support a Korean orphan back in 1972. This is not abstract theology for them but a conviction that God is good and genuinely cares and is actively engaged on behalf of the most vulnerable in every circumstance and nation.

-*David G. Boyd,* former Director of YWAM (Youth with A Mission), Hurlach, Germany 1973-1984; former Chancellor of University of the Nations, Kona, Hawaii; presently, guiding the Prayer Breakfast Movement, Wash. D.C.

II. Foreword

The remarkable feature of my friend Dixey's story is how he was passionate about God's call and purpose upon his life. As he felt the urge for this call, he left college to enlist in the Army, and ten years later, received his commission to the active duty of Army Chaplaincy. He retired as Lieutenant Colonel having served over 30 years. This alone is a history—rich of divine provision, divine help, fulfilment of divine promises, divine strength, and yet more divine possibilities.

I am always thrilled by salvation stories; I am an evangelist by calling. The salvation story captured in chapter 4 is incredible, it is a demonstration of the spirit of wisdom manifested by the Holy Spirit through Dixey, to save his life from being stoned. What a God! Yet, a more thrilling one is his impact as he preached in different places in the early years of his life. Through him, many have met the Lord and have gone ahead to become ministers of the gospel, changing many other lives subsequently. What a faith life!

The teaching of Paul in Second Corinthians chapter five and verse seven is that *"For we walk by faith [we regulate our lives and conduct ourselves by our conviction or belief respecting man's relationship to God and divine things, with trust and holy fervor; thus we walk] not by sight or appearance"* (AMPC). Faith is the firm foundation under everything that makes life worth living. Dixey is a man of faith. It is in living by faith that has punctuated and colored his life. By his invitation to read this memoir, we are called to interact with a real divinely orchestrated story.

God cares about you! God is not done with you yet! What counts beyond the very many things we shall ever do in this life, is Jesus Christ - He is our all in all. The book of James concludes it by this admonition *"…Take the old prophets as your mentors. They put up with anything, went through everything, and never once quit, all the time honoring God. What a gift life is to those who stay the course! You've heard, of course, of Job's staying power, and you know how God brought it all together for him at the end. That's because God cares, cares right down to the last detail"* (James 5:10 MSG).

I personally invite you to a life of faith - faith with actions, marked by miracles as told by my brother, Chaplain (LTC-Ret) Dixey R. Behnken.

***Dr. Ev. Charles M. Mulli,* PhD, HSC, Founder & CEO, Mully Children's Family**

Introduction

I'M A HANDS-ON TYPE of guy, always have been. When I found faith in God, it had to be hands-on. If faith didn't work, I didn't want it. I needed something real. In this book I share the joys and hardships of trying to find God.

This book is about God working with me, a stubborn, proud, resistant, rebellious and reluctant follower. Yet, when His unsurpassed love, forgiveness, grace and mercy entered the scene, my heart yielded again and again.

Marked by Miracles documents many of my life's journeys, my application of faith principles to marriage, military career, finances, parenting and retirement, notwithstanding the challenges, struggles, disappointments, doubts and failures.

God surprised me by showing up on the scene many times, with answers to prayer, divine appearances, divine provision and life-sparing angelic protection, but not always like I expected. I've labored to integrate experiencing the mysteries of life and the doldrums of reality with the supernatural realm and God's promises.

Some stories, I admit, while true, are hard to believe.

It's tough selecting, distilling and integrating snippets of my life through short time capsules called chapters. I trust you will find a balance represented here.

My wife Julie and I attended the YWAM (Youth with A Mission) missionary training at Hurlach, Germany, in 1975 and worked among missionaries for three years. I am now a retired Army Chaplain (Lieutenant Colonel) with 30 years active duty and one year in Iraq. I hold a Master of Divinity degree (Magna cum Laude) with Asbury Theological Seminary and was inducted into the *Theta Phi* Theological Honor Society in 1984. I received a Master of Science degree in *Marriage, Family and Community Development* from the University of Maryland, College Park in 1991.

I gained Clinical Membership with AAMFT (American Association of Marriage & Family Therapy) in 1998 and later became certified in Advanced EMDR (Eye Movement Desensitization and Reprocessing), treating soldiers with PTSD.

I directed three Army Family Life and Chaplain Training Centers for nine years in Fort Leonard Wood, Missouri, Republic of Panama and Fort Polk, Louisiana.

In 2015, I became the Florida Ambassador for the Mully Children's Family, Kenya.

1

Collision Decision

IN MY JUNIOR YEAR of high school, fall of 1966, I decided to visit my girlfriend, in nearby Trotwood, Ohio. I loved riding my Honda 305cc Dream motorcycle. The unbounded feeling of freedom going anywhere I wanted when I wanted was addicting. Along with two of my brothers we had all purchased our bikes as soon as we turned 16 with our life's savings from selling newspapers. My brother, Bruce, two years older, and Dean, a year younger, had both caught Honda fever. Our 13-year-old brother David, however, was still too young.

As I rounded the Wolf Creek Pike Bridge bend and sped up past the stately Antioch United Methodist Church, an unbelievable situation developed. Over a hill with a hidden dip in front of me, two cars suddenly appeared racing at least 60 mph toward me side by side taking up both lanes of the road!

~ Three Seconds to Impact~

The car passing over the double yellow line could not fall back or speed ahead fast enough. There was no escape. What lay ahead of me seemed inevitable - I would be hit unless some divine intervention occurred.

To my right was a ditch and barbed-wire fence; to the left a ditch, a parsonage, a steep hill and Wolf Creek. Taking either side would mean severe injury or death. Hitting the cars head-on was not an option. Riding the centerline down the middle of the road *between* the two cars seemed my only hope of survival.

Was I mad? Could I really accomplish that?

It is a tough decision when you only have three seconds to decide and at 16 my experience riding motorcycles was limited!

~ Two Seconds to Impact~

In a brief moment of insight, I took my hands off the handlebars to signal a split-V like a touchdown at a football game, hoping that it signaled to the two drivers my intentions so they'd give me enough room in the middle of the road to pass between them. Time ran out to brake and avoid a crash. God help me!

~ One Second to Impact ~

Amazingly the cars opened a path between them toward the road's shoulders creating a space just large enough for me to slip through the middle unscathed on my motorcycle.

~ Time's Up ~

Swoosh! My entire life flashed before me in an instant.

Relieved, I pulled my Honda to the side of the road, cut off the motor, propped out the kickstand, climbed off in a sweat, and paced around the ground trying to calm my pounding heart. Staring at the car tracks left in the gravel on both shoulders of the road, I still could not see how I'd made it through – it happened so quickly. After recovering somewhat, I said a brief fervent prayer: *Lord, thank You for that insight which worked – and for sparing my life. You must have saved me for something. I have no idea what it could be. I pray that you will show me.*

Suddenly my faith took on more meaning. Why did God allow me to live through that? My Lutheran upbringing instilled in me a belief in a God who watched over me. *Is that what just happened?*

My family had attended Providence Lutheran Church every Sunday as far back as I could remember. I was baptized as an infant, attended catechism for two years and had been confirmed as a member of the church. Chosen as the Luther League President, I sang in the choir and attended the annual youth Bible Camp—that's about it. I didn't have any special connection to God and had no idea He could be personal. I knew so little about God, I'd have much to discover.

2

In the Voice's Grip

ON AN UNUSUALLY WARM November evening of my senior year, my high school friends and I decided to ride our motorcycles to one of our favorite hangouts in Dayton, Ohio. About a year had passed since my near fatal incident on my Honda. The events of this evening would impact me in such a way as to shape my Christian faith to this very day.

My brother Dean, along with three friends and I, frequented the Hullabaloo Club on North Main Street, Dayton, Ohio, below the Forest Park Plaza to drink, dance and meet girls. For some reason, the club never carded us.

The definition of the word "hullabaloo" means: - *a clamorous noise or disturbance; - an uproar.* The very name of the dance club reflects the chilling event that occurred that night – one I would never forget.

None of us knew that The Lemon Pipers band was appearing on stage that night—the crowd went wild. This local Ohio group had gone nationwide with the song '*Green Tambourine*'. Sporting long hair, hippie style clothing, high on drugs and psychedelic lights showcasing the stage, they opened with the song that made them famous.

I wished I could grow my hair long, but my dad wouldn't allow it. I never wanted to get high on weed, but my clothing mimicked the band's. My appearance of rebellion was more of an act than real. My dad referred to me as "stiff-necked."

While drinking a beer at the bar and listening to the music, I unexpectedly heard a voice say, "*Dixey, I want you.*"

I scanned the crowd. The voice seemed to come from within me and outside of me. It came from every direction. It did not sound like a human voice, so I presumed *maybe it's God speaking.*

In our Lutheran Church, I had learned that prophets like Moses, Samuel, Jeremiah and the apostles, Peter, John and Paul had all heard God's voice at unexpected times. I'd always wondered what it would be like if I heard God's voice. As far as we were taught, God had not spoken to anyone in the last 2,000 years. *Who was I to imagine that God would add me to that list of saints? Why would God call a sinner like me? I must be imagining things. I had only drunk two beers!*

This distinctive voice spoke with a certain finality. It was not thunderous, but it resonated within my soul. I couldn't shake it. When I heard, *"Dixey, I want you,"* a second time, my heart resisted. How could I yield to a God who might want me to change my ways? I loved my lifestyle. *Wouldn't following God demand a life of sacrifice?*

I recalled how He had spoken to Moses from an obscure burning bush in the desert. Since the bush was not consumed by the fire, it attracted Moses' attention, yet I continued to resist, arguing with the voice in my mind.

I looked around to see who else was close by, turning to my friend four seats away and asked, "John, did you call me?" John said, "No." When the voice spoke that second time, I asked God: *Why would you want me? Certainly, you would not want me.* I felt like two people on the inside … one wanting to yield and one wanting to run.

I thought if I walked out the door, the voice would go away. But, when I went outside of the dance club, I still sensed the presence of God. The voice came a third time, "*Dixey, I want you.*" At that point, I concluded that it must be God's voice. No one else was near me outside.

Returning back inside the club, I thought perhaps The Lemon Pipers' music would drown out this unexpected intrusion. Then, the voice came to me a fourth time. It seemed to be an ultimatum as it came so strongly. I finally concluded that my Creator *had* actually called out to me. Looking at my watch, two hours had passed, and I'd barely noticed.

My mind filled with many questions about God. How would I seek to know Him and follow His ways? God found me, but could I discover how to find Him? *What would God possibly want with me?* I ranked in the lower third of my class with no status, wealth, genius or influence. I lived so selfishly.

In Lutheran catechism classes I learned that Martin Luther taught, "We sin every day in thought, word, and deed." Somehow, I sensed that my lifestyle would repulse God from seeking me.

This voice had affected me so deeply that I did not trust myself to drive safely home that night. Driving demands all my skills and with my head filled with this gripping voice, I could no longer concentrate well enough to drive. So, I asked my friend, John, to drive me home on my motorcycle. John usually drove us on the weekends in his hot four-on-the-floor Chevy 409 Super Sport, but he'd ridden on the back of Dean's bike with us tonight. He gladly took the keys from me and revved up the motor.

As we rode together, I told John about the voice above the roaring of the motor and rushing of the wind. When I'd asked him earlier if he had called my name, I told him I thought that God must be calling me, and I believed God had placed His hand on my life for some reason. While speaking to him from behind, I could not observe John's face or eyes. He just laughed and said, "Man, you do need another beer!"

Shaken by this encounter with a voice, I returned home at midnight, parked my Honda 305 Dream in the garage, and quietly climbed the stairs to my bedroom. I knelt down by my bed thinking if I kneeled, God would notice that my prayer was more sincere. *God, if this voice is Yours; You have found me and I heard You, but I need You to show me how to find You. Amen.*

I woke up the following morning and decided if God wanted me to follow Him, I needed to get serious and seek Him. I told my friends the reason I had acted so strangely at the club that night. It was because God was calling me. Of course, they laughed and joked about my comment.

Truthfully, they could see I was serious about my *calling.* I was in the voice's grip and decided not to go to The Hullabaloo Club anymore. At that juncture, I felt my sacrifice of not hanging out with friends would demonstrate to God that I intended to mend my sinful ways and create a continental divide between the past and the future. Over the next months, I felt my friends also distancing themselves from me as I tried to live life by different values.

In the last semester of high school, I embarked on a path toward an upward calling. However, this path did not go as smoothly and easily as I expected, nor did I become an instant saint.

To this day, there has never been a more defining event in my life that *marked me* than that night when God's voice gripped my soul. I finished my Senior year at Brookville High and graduated in May 1968.

3

Surviving an Ambush

TO CORRECTLY SET THE stage for this saga, I must flash back to my junior and senior year in high school. A friendship developed with a guy living in another town. I've changed his name and circumstances to conceal his identity. We'd met at a club, had common interests and Marti took quite a liking to me. Six years my elder, muscular, athletic, always with a ready smile, an astute businessman owning a number of companies and I perceived a good heart.

Marti helped any person in need, and he was generous to me. I became a beneficiary of his kindness.

Who knew why Marti liked me so much. We became great friends and spent a lot of time together. One time, I helped him drive some distance away to visit his brother's cabin. It was on a lake and the fishing was tops. Marti kept his boat there; it had every amenity. He loved to fish, ride his horses, trap shoot and weight lift. Sometimes he paid my way and took me to the art theater. His paintings were magnificent.

He loved working out at the gym and because I wrestled in school matches, we worked out together lifting weights. His spacious home also had gym equipment—barbells, free weights, a bench, and weight stands. He allowed me to use his equipment anytime I wanted.

We also played pool together at the local pool hall. He paid for the games, drinks, and snacks. He had a steady girlfriend who lived a few towns away. I also dated different girls from surrounding towns.

Marti enjoyed owning hotrods. One day he surprised me by driving up in a new Jaguar. His new Camaro wasn't even a year old yet. The chic 1967 E Jaguar S1 elevated his status in my eyes. It was black with beige leather interior and cost over $6,000, a hefty chunk of change in those days, but it would resell in today's market at over $60,000. He said I could use the Jag whenever I needed a car.

My naivete set me up for what could have been disastrous.

The next fall following graduation from high school, I moved to Forest City Iowa to attend Waldorf College, a Lutheran Junior College, as a pre-seminary student. I interpreted the voice I had heard the year before to mean *God was calling me to be a preacher.* My parents were thrilled when I told them my decision, but I don't think they quite comprehended the story of the voice calling me. I didn't understand it fully, either.

In my first month at Waldorf, God answered the prayer of my heart. At a chapel service, I heard an evangelist share how to know God. Ever since hearing God's voice at The Hullaballoo Club, I'd been seeking this answer and reading the Bible most intently. After the evangelist's second sermon the following evening, I walked forward and prayed to invite Jesus Christ to come into my life. I had said this prayer twice before, when I was 12 at Bible Camp and at 14 in a Billy Graham Crusade, but it didn't really seem to have much effect on me either time. However, this night was different … something changed inside. I began a living relationship with my Lord and Creator. My faith grew daily and I started sharing my faith in Bible studies across campus.

In finding Christ, I found peace, joy and assurance of God's love and forgiveness. Jesus spoke to me in my dreams. I spent hours reading the scriptures. I began understanding and following God more closely. By listening to countless sermons on the radio on Sunday mornings and hearing the teachings of great healing evangelists, I developed a broader view of denominational differences and learned to appreciate their distinctive views on God.

Seven months later, I returned home from college at Easter break. I called Marti about getting together for bowling to catch up. My life had changed so much when I received Jesus Christ as my Lord that I wanted to share the story with Marti, hoping he too could find Jesus as Lord and receive assurance of forgiveness of his sins. I had shared a little about my faith with Marti in letters but wanted to save most of the story until I got to meet with him face to face.

What I didn't know was that Marti was jealous of the time I spent away from him and how devastated he was when I left Ohio for college in Iowa. I don't think other people were aware of the strong obsession he had for me either – at least no one ever said anything to me.

I drove to his home and tried to share with Marti about my newfound faith, but he looked away from me when I spoke. As we finished the game of pool at his home, I sensed something amiss, but could not put a finger on it.

After completing my freshman year, I returned to Brookville for summer break. I called Marti about getting together. He picked me up with another new car and we went bowling at Timber Lanes, near Englewood. After three games and sharing about the changes in our lives, we got back into the car and headed home. Marti spoke of how lonely and depressed he'd become since I'd left for college and how glad he was that we had the summer ahead of us.

Marti said he wanted to pull off to the side of the road into a field, so we could just talk without interruption. I thought he might want to pray with me to receive the Lord into his life as I had shared my faith with him. He promised he would think about it. When he stopped the car and turned off the motor, he told me he needed to get something from the trunk of the car. After a few minutes I heard the trunk slam, turned my head, and saw Marti holding a small brown box as he climbed back behind the steering wheel. Handing me the box he said, "Open it."

When I saw what it was, my mouth fell open.

"Wow, Marti, why do you have this pistol?"

Marti said, "I want to give it to you, Dixey, as a gift." Well, I really didn't need a pistol – I had never spoken about wanting one. In fact, this was the first time that I'd ever seen one up close, except for looking through pawn shop showcases. It was the first time I had even held one in my hands. It read on the barrel: *Smith and Wesson .38 Special.* I've hunted with shotguns and rifles since I was 10 years old when my dad taught me to shoot, but I had no use for a pistol and was somewhat confused as to why Marti wanted me to have it.

"Why are you giving me this pistol, Marti?"

"It's because I am now convinced that God is real, and that I need Him. I would like for you to pray for me, Dixey."

"But what does that have to do with this pistol?"

"Look into the chamber," he said. An unspent round had been indented, by the firing pin. The primer had not fired.

"Well, Dixey, you're not going to believe this but," he hesitated, "I tried to kill you with that pistol."

His stammering voice tapered off as his eyes moistened.

"You did?" My eyes widened. *Should I run?*

"It's true, Dixey. I've tried on two different occasions."

He stared down at the floor, tears dripping onto his shirt. I did not know what to think. This is insane … my head was spinning. Still holding the handgun, I said "Why on earth did you want to kill me, Marti?"

"Because I saw how much you loved Jesus, and I was jealous that you were giving Him more time than you gave to me. I felt like I was losing you. I thought if I killed you, no one else would take your attention away from me. I wanted you all to myself."

My life flashed before my eyes; something was way off base here. "Marti, do you know how crazy that sounds? This is really weird stuff!"

"When I tried to kill you the first time you were home, the gun jammed … it would not fire. Afterwards, I went into the woods to practice shooting before we met again. It fired perfectly every time. I cleaned it, loaded it, and waited for us to get together again. So, when I drove us to this isolated place where no one would hear or see us, I went to the trunk of the car and pulled out this gun. I fired it again, directly at you, but it jammed again, just now."

"What the …?" the words lodged in my throat.

Marti explained, "I could not believe that this gun misfired twice now. You must have had guardian angels protecting you. God must really have a plan for your life, Dixey. I want you to have the pistol as a reminder of God's protection over your life. Will you forgive me, and pray for God to forgive me, and help me find Christ?"

I studied Marti's face and sensed genuine remorse. He sobbed heavily now. I told him, "I forgive you," as I held the .38 Special in my hands. The box of bullets was beside the gun in the box. I stared at the two cartridges with the firing pin indentations in the primer cap with both lead bullets in tact in the brass casing.

Right there, Marti prayed with me and asked Jesus into his life. He became a new creation and the Holy Spirit filled him with God's love. That was truly a life transforming day as I actually experienced God's protection from a fired handgun at point blank range.

After Marti dropped me off, I took the gun out to Somer's Farm on Air Hill Road where my brothers and I had hunted rabbits and pheasant across from Jim Steck's house during our youth. I wanted to test the gun myself and see if it was possibly a bad box of shells, or, if a defective firing pin had spared my life. Setting up a target, I loaded the weapon several times and fired each remaining bullet in the box. All rounds fired without fail. How do you explain that?

Eventually Marti married and moved out of state with his wife, Helen. Today, they have three grown children and six grandchildren. God had truly healed an emotionally unstable man. We still maintain contact with each other and pray together. Marti and Helen have been faithful followers of Jesus Christ and have financially supported their church and foreign missions.

4

They Stoned the Last Preacher who Stood Here!

I QUIT COLLEGE IN December of 1970, realizing the life of a student no longer fit me. After my three semesters of study at Waldorf, one semester at Augustana College in Sioux Falls, South Dakota, and one semester at Asbury in Wilmore, Kentucky, I could not justify borrowing more money on loans when my interest in academics fell through the floor. I liked action and my itinerant preaching work with evangelist Bruce Roy at Asbury introduced me to a new realm — revival preaching. I never consulted with my parents regarding my choices for the future.

Since turning 18, it seemed they released me to the Lord to direct me as He pleased. The only guidance they had given was where to go to my first college. After that, I was on my own. That's just how our parents raised us.

My oldest brother, Bruce, came home one day and announced he'd joined the Navy Reserves. He hadn't even spoken to mom and dad about it, either. One year later he was on a naval destroyer shelling the coasts of Vietnam.

God's calling on my life, nevertheless, kept deepening from my daily prayer, Bible studies and speaking opportunities. Back in the 70s every male 18 or older had to sign up at the draft board. The lottery determined who would go to war. But, staying in college kept me safe from the draft.

Losing my draft deferment status was the biggest hurdle that kept me from leaving college. But the lure of itinerant preaching had a greater tug on my heart and my scholastic studies lost out. The fear of the draft board calling me and going to war did cast a dark shadow over my future. I would have to deal with it sooner or later, preferably later.

* * *

No less than three weeks after quitting college, I hitchhiked from my home in Brookville, Ohio to Waco, Texas to attend a Collegiate Christian Retreat at the Grace Gospel Campgrounds (GGC). At Waldorf College, I had met Brother Robert Ewing, an itinerant charismatic evangelist who traveled the world speaking and preaching.

I kept in touch with him as he visited some 20 college campuses a year. His *Campus Fellowship* quarterly publication of his teachings and calendar listed this retreat at GGC where over 200 college students gather each year.

My dad hugged me when I left hitchhiking and put he put $100 into my hand. He told me just to use it as emergency money in case I got stuck. With only $5 of my own money left, I really wanted to see God supply all I needed. I trusted that God would help me give back the $100 to my dad once I returned home.

Once I arrived at the campgrounds, I heard that a group of 20 college students would head to Mexico City to preach on the streets, at a cost of only $50 each, in a convoy of three vehicles. I was thankful for the money my father had supplied as I really wanted to join this outreach.

This is where I met Brother Callos (pronounced 'Cai-yos') in our van. He had made this trip in previous years and offered to take me under his wing to show me the ropes of street preaching. He would be my interpreter. We shared stories and got to know each other over the three days of mountainous driving.

We arrived in Mexico City with hearts full of anticipation and prayers for God to sovereignly move upon the people. The brilliantly colored sunset appeared to radiate the promise of God's presence.

Thousands were milling around in a public square under the shadows of the opulent spires of the massive Catholic Basilica de Guadelupe Cathedral. We saw children everywhere, begging. What a contrast – the rich church and the poor people. I would preach my first street sermon next to the centuries-old Catholic edifice. With poverty all around I found it difficult to absorb the massive numbers of apparently abandoned children roaming the streets trying to survive. Perhaps it was here that God placed in my heart an incredible compassion for orphans that would one day touch the world.

At our chosen location, Brother Callos spoke for about five minutes in an effort to gather a crowd. I did not understand one word of his Spanish. I had studied Latin and French but wished now I'd studied Spanish.

I watched in awe seeing how Brother Callos' strong bass voice and dynamic mannerism easily drew people. Soon, a crowd of over 200 had merged to hear his message. Suddenly, he turned to me.

"It's time, Dixey. I you to share. Relax, don't hurry, they are all smiling and want to hear what you have to say since I told them you came all the way from the States just to speak to them. Share from your heart, speak slowly, one sentence at a time. Wait for me to translate, then follow with the next sentence. Got it?" His encouraging words allayed my fears. He smiled, "Trust God, Brother Dixey!"

I still clearly recall the message God put on my heart to share with the Mexican people. Stories told by our tour guide earlier that day in the Basilica gave me the perfect segue into my message. The huge painting on its cathedral wall displayed a 20-foot-high portrait of Jesus with bleeding knees lying in the lap of his mother, Mary (*Guadelupe*). To me, the picture portrayed Jesus penitently crawling onto the Virgin Mary's lap to gain entry into heaven. To Mexican Catholics, Mary is holy, *The Queen of Heaven*. They embrace a theology of salvation through works and penance.

In direct contrast, salvation by works is denied as the means to salvation in the gospel. Eternal life is God's free gift through 'Faith in Jesus, the Savior.' (Ephesians 1:8). You don't have to earn your way into God's favor. It broke my heart to learn how many devout Catholics there believed that parading on their knees in a procession following the *Virgin de Guadelupe* (a dark-skinned Virgin Mary) mounted on the trunk of a slow-moving car could earn their forgiveness.

When the parade of worshippers reaches the Basilica, they continue up the steps on their knees. The steps are embedded with special concrete points to purposely tear through the skin. The flesh on their knees becomes gouged out as the most devout followers of Mary leave a trail of blood behind as they ascend the stairs. This occurs on 'The Day of the Virgin Guadalupe,' (*Día de la Virgen de Guadalupe*), celebrated every December 12th.

Knowing in my heart that Jesus purchased our salvation by shedding His own blood in our place, I wanted my listeners in the square to know that Jesus already had secured our place in heaven for them through faith in His sacrifice on the Cross for us. So, I preached what was on my heart. Little did I know my statement of faith would become a death trap.

I followed the Apostle Paul's example of speaking to the Athenians on Mars Hill in Athens, appealing to their great religiosity. Brother Callos translated for me.

"You have a beautiful Basilica where all of you gather to worship God. For over 400 years your families have worshipped God on this very hill—ever since the Catholic Church recognized that *Guadelupe* appeared to Juan Diego. Inside the Basilica, you must feel awe and reverence for God—I sensed that too.

"I've travelled over 2,000 miles to share a special message with you today. It is the story of Jesus, the Son of God, the Son of the *Virgin de Guadelupe*.

Jesus willingly suffered on a Roman cross so our sins would be forgiven. In His death, Jesus paid in full the price required to cancel our sins. We can't earn it with good works. When we receive Jesus as our Savior and Lord, we are set free from sin and death. Jesus fulfilled all that is required by God's law to be saved. By receiving Jesus as Lord and Savior, we become God's children and His desires become ours. New life is a new way of thinking. We'll want to serve God from our gratitude and love, because of his Great Love for us."

At this point in my sermon, someone shouted out a question, "*¿Qué cree usted sobre la Virgin Guadelupe.*" Brother Callos leaned over and said, "Dixey, they want to know what you believe about the Virgin Mary (*Guadelupe*)." He then cautioned me to be careful how I answered the question since the last preacher standing here was severely stoned because they didn't like his answer.

I knew I needed to ask God for His divine wisdom.

My career as a street preacher could end rather abruptly right on the square of the *Basilica de Guadelupe* during my first effort at street preaching. Not being prepared for this question, the wrong answer might stir a strong reaction from this very religious crowd and my life could soon be snuffed out.

Brother Callos let me know that others were now asking "What do you have to say about *Guadelupe*?" I was trusting God to fill my mouth when I opened it.

"You ask me, what do I believe about the Virgin Mary? Well, I believe everything about the Virgin that your Bible tells you to believe! First, it says in your Bible that God sent an angel from heaven to the Virgin Mary, to tell her she was adored above all women on the earth. Everyone on the face of the earth would call her *blessed*." (Luke 1:48.) The crowd seemed pleased, nodding their heads in approval.

"Second, it says in your Bible that Mary was a virgin divinely chosen by God to bring into the world a Savior. He would be called Jesus, Emmanuel, God with us." (Matthew 1:23.) "Mary is the Mother of God."

Again, the crowd favored my answer.

"Third, it says in your Bible that when Jesus was hanging on the cross, He spoke to His most beloved disciple, the Apostle John, and told him to care for His mother when He no longer could look after her. Your Bible says John was Jesus' most beloved disciple. (Matthew 19:26.) Then Jesus was crucified on a Roman cross." The crowd again approved of my statement.

I prayed, under my breath, *Lord, how can I tie this together with the message of salvation so that they can invite Jesus into their lives?*

The Holy Spirit brought to mind the story of how believers gathered in one spot to pray for the outpouring of Pentecost in Acts of the Apostles. "*When they had entered the city, they went up to the upper room where they were staying; that is, Peter and John and James and Andrew, Philip and Thomas, Bartholomew and Matthew, James the son of Alphaeus, and Simon the Zealot, and Judas the son of James. These all with one mind were continually devoting themselves to prayer, along with the women, and Mary the mother of Jesus, and with His brothers.*" Acts 1:13,14 (NASB)

"Acts 2:1 in the Bible states that Mary was among the believers gathered on the Day of Pentecost. Filled with the Holy Spirit, believers spoke with tongues of fire in agreement with Peter when he later preached the message of salvation, 'Believe in Jesus' Resurrection.'"

"Fourth," I proclaimed, "Your Bible also says that Mary prayed to Jesus when the twelve disciples were gathered in the upper room, praying for 50 days." As I finished speaking, many in the crowd started moving toward me, led by four men.

Startled, I wondered if they were going to stone us, or if they believed what I'd told them … what I'd been given to say through the gift of the Spirit of Wisdom.

In Luke 12:11 (NASB). *"When they bring you before the synagogues and the rulers and the authorities, do not worry about how or what you are to speak in your defense, or what you are to say; for the Holy Spirit will teach you in that very hour what you ought to say."*

"Fifth, it also states in your Bible that God wants everyone to repent of their sins and pray to Jesus as Mary did in the company of Peter and the other disciples. Mary stood with Saint Peter when he preached in the streets. She heard, 'Repent and be baptized, every one of you, in the name of Jesus Christ for the forgiveness of your sins and you will receive the gift of the Holy Spirit.'" (Acts 2:38 (NIV). "I believe that Mary wants you to do what she did."

Four men in leather jackets came forward and stood prominently in front of me. "Can we help you?" I asked.

One of them leaned over to us and softly said, "How do we receive forgiveness for our sins?" Before I could answer back through Brother Callos, the four men kneeled down right in front of me, heads bowed. I then had the privilege of leading them in a prayer of repentance, inviting Jesus Christ into their hearts. They repeated each phrase, *aloud*, together as Brother Callos interpreted for me. Then, I placed my hand upon their heads and asked Jesus to fill them with the Holy Spirit.

Many in the crowd joined with them in repeating the prayer of forgiveness. I asked them if they wanted to worship Jesus the same way the Virgin Mary had.

Many knelt and prayed with us.

I rejoice that God anointed my message that day. Those saved by grace embraced the true knowledge of who Jesus Christ really is. Brother Callos and I introduced these new believers to members of a nearby local church where they would have the opportunity to join the fellowship. In time, they would grow in their faith, learn more about the Bible, and receive discipleship materials.

The kingdom of heaven increased by some 20 souls that night.

We met with them each day before leaving the city and they received training in their newfound faith. I established a long-term friendship with one of the four, Hector Perez Chavez. Over the next two years through writing letters, I encouraged and discipled him in the Lord. He spoke English quite well and became a street evangelist, leading many to Jesus after I left Mexico City.

5

California! Here we Come!

BROTHER CALLOS AND I had become very close during this evangelistic trip to Mexico. So, when he asked if I would like to also travel through Texas, New Mexico, Arizona, Nevada and on to Southern California together to preach at a several churches, I took the chance.

I was aware that 'The Jesus People' movement was still going strong and rapidly growing at this time in 1971. I also wanted to visit my relatives. Mom's brother, Uncle Dick and Aunt Dottie who lived in Los Angeles with my cousins. I'd never had a chance to visit them, never having been in California before.

Brother Callos and I began our journey, traveling through Texas and then New Mexico. As we drove down Route 10 outside of Albuquerque, I noticed the red flashing of the van's engine light next to the odometer. I mentioned it to Brother Callos, but he was not concerned.

"Oh, we will just trust God to heal whatever is going on with the motor." He placed his hand on the dashboard saying, "Dear Jesus, we pray that You will heal our motor, right now, in Jesus' name we ask, Amen." He grinned and assured me it would be all right. I wasn't so sure. Red lights flip on for a reason and it continued brightly lit after his prayer ended.

I countered, "Shouldn't we at least stop and see what is going on before we get out into the desert and away from the city?"

He threw up a hand. "Nothing to worry about … you must have faith, my friend. God will take care of us."

Brother Callos kept driving on into the night as we watched a spectacular desert sunset. About an hour and a half later, I woke up feeling vibrations from the stones and rocks on the shoulder of the interstate. We slowed and stopped as the van's headlights faded into almost nothing. Apparently, the alternator failed to recharge the battery as I had feared. I looked for Brother Callos' response.

"The motor started sputtering and then just quit altogether. We could go to sleep and pray that God sends us some help in the morning."

Snow was falling and I didn't have a clue what to expect. It was my first time in New Mexico. We put on our coats, crawled into our sleeping bags, zipped them up and snoozed till morning. After waking, we decided first to lay our hands on the van and pray for it to run, but to no avail. The battery did not even have enough juice to turn the motor over.

I got out of the van and walked about a hundred yards to our rear, intent on flagging down someone who could assist us in finding a mechanic. I genuinely wanted to believe that God would work a miracle like Brother Callos had promised, but I struggled with the idea, thinking God gave us common sense for a reason. Yet, I did not want to spoil the experience of faith achieving a miracle if abandoning my reasoning was a pre-requisite.

It turned out that the first car that came by, pulled over. The driver 'happened' to be the son of a mechanic and his father's shop was only 20 miles away! He would be glad to remove the alternator for us, drive us to his dad's shop, get it repaired, then return us to the van and have us on our way by tomorrow. We met his father, Juan, who demonstrated for us how to repair the alternator.

Juan said: "You never know when you might need to do this yourselves someday. I'll just re-grind the armature and replace the worn brushes."

That evening, Brother Callos gave us a Bible study, and we stayed up late talking about the ways of God.

The next morning both father and son drove us back to the van to check out the rest of our motor, reinstall the alternator, and make sure everything was working. We jumped the battery cables to their tow truck battery. The motor started and we set off to California again.

In retrospect, I pondered if God did heal the motor – just in a different way than I expected. He did not touch it instantly to make it perfect, but we encountered the most wonderful mechanically skilled assistance possible, from men whom we now knew as brothers in the Lord.

I began to consider how God heals in different ways. What people often call coincidences … could they actually be miracles? My spiritual education entered a new phase as a result of my association with Brother Callos. Truly, he must have been sent to help me.

After dropping me off at my Uncle Dick's in Tustin, California, Brother Callos headed south to Tijuana – his next preaching mission; that was the last time I saw him. I stayed with my cousins for three weeks and renewed our distant relationships.

At a Bible study Uncle Dick arranged, his best friend and estranged son reconciled after years of hatred toward each other. God used the message I spoke on forgiveness to melt away the years of bitterness and restored their whole family

* * *

I greatly enjoyed flying with Uncle Dick in his Ponderosa as he flew around delivering aircraft parts all over L.A. county. After some instruction with the controls on the control wheel, ailerons, elevators and rudder, Uncle

Dick said, "Take over, Dixey!" I knew after a few moments that I, too, would get my pilot's license someday.

Before heading to my next destination, the phone rang. "Hey, Dixey, your dad is on the line."

It's the first time I talked to my parents since I'd left. After a bit of catching up, dad said, "Oh, I have a letter here for you from Uncle Sam." I froze. I knew that I would eventually get one. It took Uncle Sam nine months to get to my lottery number: **55**. I just lost control of my entire future and will probably be sent to Vietnam.

When I told Uncle Dick, he asked me if I would report to the draft board. I told him what I told dad. "If they don't know where I am, I can't get the letter, just keep it until I get home. Tell them you don't know where I am if they call." I'd decided a long time ago, I will not dodge the draft. But that doesn't mean I can't delay it a little while.

* * *

The thought of going to war now loomed gloomily over me as I hitchhiked from Tustin to Sunnyvale, California. I encountered a vast spider web of interstate highways going through Los Angeles. Hitchhiking through LA proved quite a task. The perplexing concrete interstate maze took me two full days just to get through the 70-mile stretch. Then, one kind driver picked me up and took me all the way to my uncle's home.

* * *

One of my close brushes with death, of the 23+ times I have come face to face with death, occurred at the age of 20 while staying with my mom's brother, Uncle Kenny's
family.

After several Bible Studies with my cousin's friends, Craig, whom I'd met earlier, invited me to go bodysurfing with him. His Olympic stature should have given me a clue, but I missed it. He said bodysuits would keep us warm and that he goes body- surfing all the time. February's sea swells surpass most of the other months of the year.

Going bodysurfing sounded like a real blast, but I had never even seen the ocean before. I loved adventure and was always up for a challenge. As we pulled into the parking lot some 100 feet above a cliff over the vast azure Pacific, my breath hastened. The enormous waves rolled in over 10 feet high. They crashed upon monstrous boulders the size of small houses lining the almost vertical rock wall.

After putting on our wetsuits, we began descending to the sea. My cousins watched from the car. The water was fifty degrees and once in, it would only be a few moments before my body heat would warm up the trapped water between my skin and the body-suit.

Craig said" Follow my lead," and dove into the water, swimming off like a sea otter. When I jumped into the water right after the next wave, Craig was already out about 100 feet. Hundreds of freezing needles pierced my skin as the water filled my body suit, numbing my entire body. The icy assault shocked me as I tried to stroke and kick while holding the raft tightly under me with one arm. Before I could make my way out, a wave immersed me. Its power overwhelmed me so much that my fierce grab penetrated right through the seam of the raft. "Boom!" I looked back from where I had launched, and my courage deflated just as fast as my body raft. I saw nothing but the huge crashing waves.

I shouted out, "Devil, you are not going to get me," trying to resist the creeping paralyzing fear. *Was this how it would all end?* I prayed: "Lord, how do I survive this?" I heard a reasoning analysis of my situation, almost as if I had an instructor coaching me.

Gauge the speed of the returning waves. Observe which place that each wave smashes upon the highest point of the rock. Position yourself in the wave at that same place where the preceding wave landed highest on the rock. As it washes away, it will drop you upon the rock. That way it will not smash you between the waves and the boulders.

"The words were specific and clear, but could I manage to do that? I only had one attempt, as my strength waned. I prayed and made my best effort to swim as hard as I could and catch the wave at the right place. Surprisingly, it all worked out just like I heard from the voice. There were enough rivulets and holes on the boulder to grip onto. Now, I only had to jump back into the water toward the rock wall and beat the next wave to make it to the top of the next boulder on the beach along the rock wall.

"I made it!" I cried out to Craig above the roaring of the surf, "I'm okay!" My cousins had watched the whole episode helplessly from above. They'd been praying for me from the moment they saw my body raft explode. When Craig, the expert swimmer, made it up the rock wall back to the car, he said, "Dixey, I am an atheist, but if I have ever had any reason to believe in God, you gave me one today. I thought you were a dead man. Your escape was a miracle!" I had thought that I was a goner too, but God had seen it fit to help me survive.

After spending a few weeks with my Uncle Kenny and cousins, I hitched to Sacramento. When I saw a freight train heading East, I decided to hop on. It ended up taking me through the Salt Lake Flats and on to Salt Lake City, Utah where I jumped off. Some rides were short, some long. I enjoyed sharing my stories and faith with travelers who picked me up. Many times, they would pray with me when they dropped me off, sometimes asking Jesus to come into their lives.

My longest jaunt with one person was from Rock Springs, Wyoming, to Minneapolis, Minnesota. Traveling 24 hours through a blinding snow blizzard over 1,000 miles, I was shocked at the speed and traction of the VW bug with its snow tires. It never once failed to deliver when we had to punch through long snowdrifts.

I finally arrived at the home of Cathy Bock, an acquaintance from my Waldorf College days who lived in Minneapolis. I attended church with her and met her pastor. He invited me to speak at their Lutheran youth retreat the following week about my travels and adventures in faith.

At the end of the retreat, they took an offering and gave me a gift of $100 for my future travels. I laid this money aside to repay my father for his initial contribution to help me on my way. God answered my prayers to pay dad back. I headed from Cathy's home down to St. Olaf College.

6

A Lifetime Impact

AFTER SPENDING A FEW days with Jim Woodruff at St. Olaf College in Northfield, Minnesota and renewing our friendship from my Waldorf days, I headed out the door to begin hitchhiking. Thankfully, I now wore the pair of brand-new cowboy boots Jim had given me after he saw my thin-soled, hole-filled shoes. I discovered that God oversees even the smallest matters. The big surprise to me was that Jim told me he'd considered giving them to me three days before I arrived.

* * *

I set my sights on Cedar Rapids, Iowa. My trip held no surprises the next 300 miles. It left too much time to wonder about the war and if I am walking toward my death during the long hours of holding out my thumb waiting for cars along the side of the road. I traveled south-south-east through the lingering spring snows of Minnesota and Iowa. As I encountered more snow, I remembered the blizzard when I left home over three months ago. Snow usually covers the ground from Thanksgiving to Easter in this northern region.

I arrived at my destination and phoned Barb Katcher, a good friend I led to Christ at Waldorf College back in 1969. She offered her family's home for a few days rest over. She'd received a couple of letters from me describing my adventures hitchhiking across the nation and she was excited to hear about God's faithfulness in more detail. To prepare for my arrival, she invited many high school friends and her brother, Rex, to come to a Bible study where I would speak.

At our meeting we sang many joyful songs, shared scripture, and spoke about the crowd who might have stoned me while preaching in Mexico City ... one of my favorite stories to share to this day. God's instantaneous download of wisdom most likely saved my life in Mexico.

Barb's spirit was touched deeply and from that night a *calling* began to grow in her heart to share her faith in God with Hispanic people. I marvel at how Jesus included all humanity when he mandated that his disciples go out to all nations preaching the gospel (Matthew 28:18). God also moved in a special way over her brother, Rex, as he prayed to receive Christ as his Lord and Savior.

The following evening Barb planned for us to go to a roller-skating rink to enjoy a relaxing time together as we both loved skating. While skating around the rink, I thought about sharing my faith with the crowd during intermission. People should know how to find eternal life.

After everyone sang and danced the Hokey Pokey song, *Stick your right leg in, stick your right leg out.....* I asked the rink manager for permission to speak a few minutes and surprisingly he said yes. They turned on the overhead lights and announced that I had hitchhiked over 4,000 miles preaching the gospel and would like to share a few experiences about the trustworthiness of God. When I concluded some eight minutes later and offered an invitation, five young people came forward to invite Christ into their lives. On the way home, Barb and her friends all rejoiced that God is faithful to change people's lives, even in a roller skating rink.

When I called Barb while writing this story to ensure the facts were correct, she told me that her brother, Rex, had become a Lutheran pastor and was pastoring a church in Illinois. Barb also shared that a year after my visit, she went to Mexico on a mission trip while still in college. There she met an Argentinian evangelist named Henry Tolopilo. They became close friends, later married and spent over 10 years in mission work in Mexico where she learned to speak fluent Spanish.

Now Barb's husband is the pastor to the Hispanic congregation at John MacAuthur's Church in Sun Valley, California. Henry and Barb's four adult children are all serving the Lord and leading Christian ministries in their community. The lifetime impact of a single gospel message totally transforms a person's future. Now, Barb's grandchildren are worshipping the Lord!

* * *

Every place I have ventured during my ministry, God has accomplished marvelous wonders of His grace and mercy in so many unique ways.

In late March 1971, close to my journey's end, I pondered what lay ahead. Certainly, God would continue to be faithful and unravel the deepest mysteries of His will and character by performing signs and miracles to confirm His holy word.

One of the most important points of learning about miracles is that believing in Jesus is esteemed over and above miracles. He is of highest significance and eternal value. Jesus used miracles to lead people to 'Believe in Him.'

Believing is primary; miracles are secondary. John 14:11 (NASB). "Believe me when I say that I am in the Father and the Father is in me. Or at least believe on the evidence of the works themselves." We can do without miracles, they will pass, but we cannot do without true living faith. Nevertheless, I still had this urge to see miracles, too.

7

Does God Heal?

UPON RETURNING HOME from my 5,000-mile hitchhiking adventure in the first week of April 1971, I had the great pleasure of handing my dad a plastic bag of change making up one hundred dollars to the penny. He smiled and tucked it away.

In turn my dad handed me an unopened letter to Dixey Behnken, #55 from the draft board. My dad had served in the Navy during WWII. The Vietnam War needed good young men. "It's every man's duty to serve his country," dad said.

When I reported to the draft board, I discovered that they could send me to Germany instead of Vietnam, *if* I signed a three-year contract. I gladly exchanged an additional year of my life in order *not* to get drafted to 'Nam for two years. I had lost friends to the war. Germany would be like a gift compared to going there. Also, discovering our family history intrigued me. My father's and mother's parents were German and had migrated to the States in the 1890s-1900s from the city of Bremen.

Maybe I would get the chance to reconnect with the Behnken families of our roots. My college German language courses could help me facilitate that. But first, I had a report date to Basic Training at Ft. Campbell, Kentucky on June 21, 1971.

With three months of freedom before putting on the OD green fatigues, my brother Bruce and I planned a trip before Easter. We began lining up a group of students in Brookville, Ohio to take to another Christian Collegiate Retreat to Waco, Texas, where I'd hitched to four months earlier.

My brother's large Dodge van perfectly fit our needs for the trip. I had several friends living near Columbus I thought would be interested in attending, one of them being Vicki Strong. We had met in our mid-teens at the Lutheran Memorial Camp in Fulton, Ohio. After graduating high school, we dated and sometimes discussed a closer relationship, but it did not turn into a lifetime romance – just a close friendship. Vicki agreed to go with us (and four others) over Easter break. She had been born with a congenital birth condition affecting her back. While we were at the collegiate retreat in Waco, God did something special and amazing.

I called Vicki while writing this book and she agreed that I could relate how God worked in her life at the retreat. She sent me these words.

The trip to Waco, Texas was a miracle. My parents would never have let me go so far away. So, getting their permission would occur only by the Lord's intervention. I went because many of my college friends were going to Florida and I thought that Texas would also be a good enough place to get a good suntan. I would love the road trip with Dixey, his brother, Bruce, and friends. More than I ever expected, God had bigger things than I could have dreamed. After arriving at Grace Gospel Campgrounds in Waco, getting bed assignments and eating dinner with a group of over 200 students from 20 colleges, I went to attend the evening revival meeting with Dixey. The atmosphere and service were new to me. It was nothing like I had seen in all my life in the Lutheran Church.

After the meeting ended, I was eager to get a good night's rest and recover from the long drive down. But that was not to be. After pulling up my covers and closing my eyes, I could hear loud muffled voices coming through the walls. I discovered that my bed was on the other side of a wall from the sanctuary pulpit, where people continued praying at the altar all night long. You would have thought God must be deaf, they cried out so loudly. I thought you only prayed at meals and bedtime. The prayers kept me awake almost the whole night.

Dixey knew I had terrible back pain from the time I was small. I'd lived with spina bifida and scoliosis, also diastematomyelia which is a double spinal cord. I was supposed to be twins.

After breakfast, about 30 of us gathered around a circle at a campfire the next morning, taking turns to pray. Dixey turned and asked me if I would like prayer for my back. I paused thinking for a moment, "Whatever."

Pain is all that I had ever known and I knew the pain would always be there. So, I said, "Well, I guess it couldn't hurt." Dixey placed his hand in the middle of my back, raised his other hand up to God, and began praying aloud for Him to heal my back. I was not familiar with people raising their hands when they prayed or praying aloud extemporaneously in a group. What the heck, if this works, that's okay with me. After he prayed, nothing felt different.

During the rest of that day, we attended different meetings and teaching sessions. I remember loving the singing during the times of worship. That night I went to bed and suddenly realized: "I have no pain!" This really surprised me. I knew that certainly by morning I would be hurting again. But, to my amazement, when I awoke my back didn't hurt at all!

God had truly healed me. During that week, it was the healing that brought me to the realization that God was interested in me personally. I knew I needed a Savior and began to follow Jesus that week through the transformation of my healing. I now have three children and grandchildren. The pain has never returned. God has blessed my life so much!

When Vicki told me that God healed her in the last 24 hours, we rejoiced. Would I become a healing evangelist like the great biblical healers? I knew it was possible through the power of prayer for Vicki to be healed, but I had never witnessed an instantaneous healing—especially through *my* prayers..

I had only read stories before of how God used Kathryn Kuhlman, Oral Roberts, John Osteen and T. L. Osborn. I previously questioned if God would use me when I sensed an urgency to pray for the healing of others. I didn't know if I was just creating my own mental gymnastics of magical thinking or realizing that some of us actually do have true gifts from God for the physical healing of others.

Vicki's healing led me one step closer to believing God for greater healings and miraculous releases. The time would come for even more of God's supernatural action in my life. I hungered for more, yet doubting seemed a reoccurring habit. My reluctance to trust God in my calling competed with obedience and stepping out in blind faith. It would take some years of spiritual maturing before I understood how to navigate the pathway separating the natural and the supernatural.

8

Flight of Destiny

ON JUNE 21, 1971, I ENTERED Boot Camp, the Army's Basic Training. I trained two months at Ft. Campbell, Kentucky as a Soldier and then two months at Ft. Knox, Kentucky as a Tanker. I headed off to Germany in the height of the Vietnam war.

On the day before I shipped off to Europe, November 5, 1971, my brother Bruce invited me to speak at a Bible study in Eaton, Ohio. That's where I met a beautiful high school cheerleader senior, Julie Kiracofe. Man, she had an effect on me like no other woman. After having only spoken with her for five minutes that evening, I wondered where this might lead. I couldn't stay long afterward because I had to head home to pack and catch an early flight. I did not initiate giving her my address because I would be thousands of miles away and that's not a good basis for a relationship. Besides, I did not want to appear too forward. I hoped our meeting had the same effect on her, but I didn't know.

I made this a matter of prayer. If God wanted *us* to happen, He would do it.

I had been in Germany for three weeks, when I received a letter. The envelope was decorated with colorful artistic designs. The return address said Julianne Kiracofe. She wrote me! She had called my brother Bruce to get my address the morning after our meeting.

Over the course of the next year and a half, three major events occurred which proved to have a powerful influence over my entire future.

* * *

Shortly after arriving at Storck Barracks, Illesheim, 1-13th Armor Battalion, I received a letter from the David Livingston Missionary Foundation encouraging me to support orphans. I felt a deep longing to support an orphan. I committed $15 a month to sponsor Bong Kyu Lee, a six-year-old Korean boy. Watching starving orphans begging on the streets in Mexico City at the beginning of that year touched me more deeply than I first realized. It would affect my entire future.

* * *

In September 1972, my unit selected me as the battalion's most outstanding Soldier. They rewarded me with three tickets to the Munich Olympic Games and a round-trip train ticket for three days. At the Olympics I met young people from Youth with A Mission (YWAM). They had just purchased a castle to the South of Augsburg for their new headquarters. There, I would learn more about faith, healing and miracles.

* * *

For the last 18 months, Julie and I had communicated via snail mail (letters, posted one-way by air mail that took over 10 days).

Our love burned like fire, but was it for real?

In May 1973, I flew to Miami, FL. where Julie attended college to spend two weeks with Julie to find out if she was *the one*. We enjoyed each other's company so much that we entertained the idea of Julie flying back to Germany with me. She could work in missions and live at the YWAM castle located 120 miles from my base. I could drive to visit her on weekends, giving us the time needed to discover if we might have a future together. When we checked the airlines to see if she could get a seat with me on my return flight, we were elated to find an open seat!

Julie's parents gave her their approval and presented her with a new suitcase, a symbol of their blessing. All we needed now was the YWAM base director (David Boyd's) permission for Julie to work and live at Hurlach Castle. We called him and he gladly welcomed Julie's visit.

The next day, we stepped onto our *flight of destiny*.

Every weekend of the next four months I made trips from Storck Barracks to the castle to spend time with Julie. Our love grew stronger with each weekend; I finally asked Julie:

"Would you marry me?" She closed her eyes, paused and looked down.

"Yes, with one condition."

"Oh, what's the condition?"

"That you call my dad and ask him for my hand in marriage."

I smiled and agreed.

Our call to her father went as planned but was a little awkward. Long distance calls to the states cost over $4.00 a minute. I could only afford to call him on HAM radio. The HAM operator and a long-distance operator had to operate two toggle switches simultaneously to reverse the one-way HAM conversations. When we each stopped speaking, we had to say, "Over" to key the toggle switch. Plus, the two operators had to listen in on the private conversation. Her dad responded, "Well if you're asking for her hand, you had better take the rest of her." The operators laughed before I could.

After getting her dad's permission, Julie made plans to return back to the States in October so she could make preparations for the wedding. We pledged our vows in a small country church on December 22, 1973. We returned back to Germany after New Year's Day for my remaining year in the Army.

9

Four Eyes!

DURING OUR FIRST YEAR of marriage, Julie and I dealt with the types of problems common to newlyweds. The Army deployed me for field duty and tank qualification four of our first six months of marriage. This absence put a great strain on our marriage.

David and Carol Boyd, the Hurlach Castle YWAM leaders (who had become close confidants during our dating period) also helped us through our marriage struggles. We are greatly indebted to them for sharing their wisdom with us.

.* * *

After my separation from the Army, December 1974, I swore that I would never wear a green uniform again, words I eventually would eat. The YWAM castle became our new home. We had decided to enroll in the eight-month YWAM missionary training school. The first three months were basically lectures, on Biblical studies by visiting evangelists and missionaries. The second three months of this training afforded us the opportunity to visit many European, Middle East and Eastern Bloc nations as part of our training. The last two months were a Summer of Service.

The first six weeks of our travels had already taken our 40 students through Austria, Italy, Greece, Israel, Rhodes, and now Turkey. As convoy leader, chief mechanic and lead bus driver for the three-month journey through the Middle East, we headed out again on the next leg with our four vehicles from Izmir on the Mediterranean Sea to Ankara, almost in the center of Turkey.

We often traveled at night to save time and finances, but that decision sometimes led us into precarious conditions. One night at 2:30 a.m., rain was peppering down and passing cars splashed oil slicks from the road up onto my windshield, making it incredibly difficult to see anything in front of me.

I had already stopped twice in the rain to wipe off the messy windshield with a rag so I could see the road better to continue driving. As we bounced over the numerous potholes on the road, Bob Jennings, my backup driver, screamed "Dixey, Stop! Now!" Without hesitating and in blind trust, I slammed on the brakes as hard as I could. The wheels locked and we skidded to a halt.

Everyone asleep in their seats were jolted awake and slid forward, with some tumbling into the aisles of the bus. They all wanted to know "What's wrong – is everything okay?" Thankfully, no one was hurt.

Just three feet in front of us was an old Turkish man steering a wooden cart pulled by two oxen. The cart had no taillights, no reflectors and no flags of warning of any nature. I had not seen the oxcart because the shining lights of oncoming cars blinded my vision through the oil-soaked sheen on the windshield.

The window on the passenger side had allowed Bob a clearer view of the road ahead. Thanks to his acute observation and fast warning, our prayers for travel protection averted a tragedy. I dread thinking what would have happened if Bob was asleep in the passenger seat that night. Four eyes are always better than two … a lesson we tried to employ on the remainder of our travels while driving at night.

10

Date with the Soviet Border

AFTER SPENDING A WEEK in Ankara and two weeks in Istanbul, Turkey for training with the British and Swiss YWAM schools, we prepared for our overnight departure to keep our border crossing appointment at the Soviet border. It was June 1st, 1975. We said our goodbyes to new and old friends in Istanbul and drove through Bulgaria to Bucharest, Romania. The terrain was remote and forested with beautiful fir trees. I had scheduled to arrive at the Communist border crossing at Leuşeni, Romania/Moldavia within 24 hours from our start.

We affectionately dubbed our 40 passenger Mercedes touring bus, 'Katy' as her license plate was KT46. Katy quietly hummed along; the sound of her diesel motor giving me a reassuring confidence that all would go well as everyone settled in for the long journey.

We departed at 8 a.m. The border checkpoint lay some 600 miles ahead. We had to be 'on time' in order to pass through customs at the infamous 'Iron Curtain' (a title Winston Churchill gave the Soviet Union in 1946). That inclusive name specified neighboring satellite countries within the Soviet Union. All were barricaded from Western thought, military, spiritual, political influence and foreign travel.

If we missed our deadline, the border point would refuse our entry.

Of all the times we needed Katy *not* to break down, this was it. Our bus had never failed us before. Cautiously, I had built a three-hour buffer into our itinerary for unexpected events that might delay us. Later in the day we took our time to pause since everything had gone so smoothly. We grabbed a nice nap, did some sightseeing and light shopping in a quaint Romanian village.

All four vehicle drivers had their oil changed and radiators checked. A GPS would have been nice back in those days. I was familiar with all-night driving but maneuvering through Iron Curtain countries at night was quite another task.

The main roads of first world nations made these Bulgarian main roads look like something from the 1940s Oklahoma dust bowl; potholed and packed dirt. Would our tires endure the extreme demands of the torturous roads?

My praying jumped up a notch. I'm sure our group prayed for me as well, when they saw the treacherous roads.

Our baggage and food supplies were stored in the secondhand repurposed Mercedes postal truck for the next month's supplies as we would travel through the Soviet Union, Poland, and East Germany. With 35 missionaries from eight nations traveling together, we disguised our group's name so as not to disclose the real purpose of our trip into the Communist nations.

We called our group *"School of Culture"*, a pseudonym we used when we applied for our visas three months earlier. Had the Intourist Bureau learned of our evangelistic orientation, they would have refused visa approval.

It seemed they feared the Bible more than the bullet.

Traveling into Communist Bloc countries and the Soviet Union is not something people often dream of doing. Back in those days, one would not normally travel there for a vacation or tourism. Fear of Soviet attack across Europe kept the U.S. government on high alert and a Division of our tanks positioned on the Czech and East German border. Our military presence signified our commitment to fight until death to keep Europe open and free. Fear and foreboding accompanied any visit.

You might never come back.

Eighteen Hours to the Soviet Border

The Leușeni border crossing checkpoint allowing us to enter the Soviet Union took on special importance for our group since we had prepared well through classes to share the gospel in a land that embraced atheism. The Bible is contraband in the Soviet Union. The gospel message is unwelcome, since officially there is no God. To better understand the culture, we'd read the books, 'God's Smuggler' and 'The Ethics of Smuggling' authored by Brother Andrew. For decades, he'd smuggled Bibles into many Communist nations out of his home in Holland.

Before continuing on, we passed out our 35 Russian Bibles to everyone in our group, which we hid in our luggage. By law, tourists were allowed to bring only one Bible. This proved to be a problem later at the border.

Unrelenting, the Soviets would fail to live up to their own laws.

Another problem troubling us involved our five YWAM students from South Africa. The Soviet Intourist Bureau withheld their travel visas due to poor diplomatic relation problems with South Africa. We had hoped their visas would be sent ahead of us to Istanbul. They never arrived. So, we had to shift the five South Africans to our YWAM Swiss School of Evangelism's bus where they would travel into Yugoslavia.

Twelve Hours to the Soviet Border

My fervent prayer, *Lord help us make it to the Iron Curtain border on time* took on new meaning as I glanced down at the temperature motor gauge on the dashboard. Out of habit, I made it a point to check the motor gauges and instrument panel every five minutes or so. About half-way to our destination, the temperature gauge had risen above the red line, the boiling point of 100 degrees Celsius, bad news indeed! I popped on the four-way emergency blinkers, put Katy into neutral, signaled the convoy we were stopping, and coasted safely off to the side of the road and shut down the motor. *What could be wrong?*

My mechanic and maintenance training from repairing tanks, tracked vehicles, trucks, and jeeps from my Army days came in handy. I rushed to the motor compartment in the back. Steam billowed out as I opened the containment door. After it dissipated, I began searching for the problem. I spied a small bead of steam coming from between the copper coils about three inches below the top center of the radiator.

From the force of steam exiting a small hole in the copper cooling tubing, shreds of tiny pieces of copper foil had blown out from the neatly packaged alignment. It looked as if a .45 caliber bullet had torn through one side of the coils and blown them out. Fortunately, John Babcock, the master mechanic at the castle who operated our auto maintenance shop, had given me a box of all types of assorted fixer-up supplies before we left.

I located a roll of bailing wire, a sparkplug and some very fast-setting waterproof cement to jam the spark plug into the hole and use the bailing wire to hold the spark plug in place in the hole. Secondly, I wrapped strands of wire around the radiator to tighten the wire down around the spark plug by twisting a vise grip. Next, I poured the cement over the hole as I screwed in the spark plug. This way it just might provide enough pressure to keep the water from boiling out of the radiator. I had no idea how much pressure a radiator created or if this would even hold.

Where on earth would I find a replacement radiator for a 20-year-old Mercedes Benz bus in a Communist nation? We had passed only one gas station every 50 to 75 miles while coming from Istanbul. I sure hoped my repairs would work satisfactorily. Fortunately, John Babcock had also placed several gallons of spare antifreeze in the supply box in our Mercedes tent and food hauling truck.

We began our journey again. Bob Jennings rotated driving shifts with me every two hours during the night so we could catch up on sleep. With every shift change we would recheck the repair work on the radiator. Relieved to see that the wire-tightened-glued-spark plug fix held fast with no leaks, we trudged on.

Our travel through the rolling country forests of evergreens provided a sense of calm and peacefulness. Three hundred miles were behind us since the breakdown repair. Thank God, almost there.

Dixey R. Behnken

Five Minutes till Showtime

Razor and barbed-wire strung over 20-foot-high fences and armed guards loomed out in the distance. We had reached our last half-mile before the border crossing. Just as I slowed our approach, I noticed through the rear mirror that the radiator was spewing clouds of white steam out the diesel motor's air vent at the rear of the bus, like before. I glanced at the temperature gauge. Red-lined at 100 degrees Celsius, again! Something was definitely wrong.

I turned off the motor and coasted downhill to the heavily reinforced barbed wire gate crossing the road. There stood two border guards with machine guns slung over their shoulders on patrol. Hoping the motor had not blown, I pulled the emergency brake, swung open the door and dashed outside to check on our problem. At my sudden action, the Soviet guards became very agitated. They waved their automatic machine guns at me, screaming, "*возвратитесь к автобусу!*" I deciphered to mean, "Get back in the bus!" I obeyed, post haste!

The guards ran toward us and followed me aboard. Then, after calling the customs officials to get clearance, they asked to see our passports. I tried to explain to them why I needed to get out and check the motor by pointing at the temp gauge, but the language barrier prevented them from understanding.

Fortunately, we had stopped uphill from the border checkpoint below. When the guards were satisfied with our passports and signaled for us to enter through the open gate, I merely released the brakes and rolled downhill, coasting across the border into the Soviet Union. We came to a stop at the front door of the Intourist Bureau. We'd made it safely across, and, on time. "Praise the Lord!"

What an intense time the last 12 hours had been. I recalled asking the Lord earlier, *Help us, Lord, to get to the Leușeni check point on time at the Russian border. We will all be so grateful.* I realized that the Lord had answered my prayer exactly as I had prayed. Our bus had never failed us until this point; always starting, always humming along, never missing a beat. Even the poor grade diesel fuel of third world nations had not affected her dependability. Our timely arrival was God's miracle to me.

While everybody in our group processed through customs and passports, I went back to the engine compartment of our bus to re-rig a second fix to the leaking radiator. We would have to make it more than 300 miles to reach Kiev in the Ukraine before we could find a radiator repair shop. They did not have a NAPA Auto Parts store in every town where you could walk in to get an after-market remanufactured radiator like in the States! Little did I realize then that the damaged radiator would be the least of my worries on our trip to Kiev.

11

Slip Sliding Away

AT THE LEUSENI CHECKPOINT, our four vehicles in the convoy lined up as we prepared to depart customs between the no man's land of the Leuşeni, Romania and the Moldavian border crossing checkpoint. We had traveled in our convoy for the last 2,400 miles. We processed through customs, changed our currency into Russian rubles, and bought enough 10-liter diesel vouchers for the entire trip to Moscow and our return to the Polish border through Brest, Belarus (White Russia). Our travels would take us over 1,320 miles through the Soviet Union.

With passports and visas in hand, Julie smiled at me as she climbed into our bus and modeled the beautiful cashmere shawl that she had purchased at the Intourist souvenir shop. When the bus reloaded with everyone aboard, we discovered that the customs' officials had confiscated 30 of the 35 Russian Bibles during their inspections. At least five Bibles got through. Russian Bibles were so scarce that they sold for the price of a cow in the black market.

Our 35 missionaries had suspicions about our assigned guide, Nadia, who took the front seat. After all, the Soviet Union forbid evangelism. The Intourist Bureau required Nadia to ride with us for our entire journey throughout the Soviet Union. We wondered if she really came along just to spy on us. It turns out that we really needed her translation and navigation abilities, regardless.

With Soviet pride, Nadia brightly welcomed us into her native country. She would give us history lessons as we drove through and introduced us to our appointed tour guides at each major city. She boasted about how valiantly her country fought against the Nazis in WWII. She insured we would watch the *Komsomol* (Leninist Communist Youth League) honor guard formations of twelve to fifteen-year-old's marching in front of every WWII War Monument of each Soviet city we passed through.

Our diesel motor kept humming as I hoped it would.

The sun had set; we would soon be in Kiev within a few hours. In these northern latitudes it did not get dark until after 11 p.m. Practically everyone on the bus fell fast asleep. We were all tired as we traveled straight through our second night. Drops of rain pelted the windshield so I turned on the wipers.

Phillip Hampe, our retired Air Force Chaplain and resident historian rode shotgun in the second seat next to Nadia. As I drove on toward Kiev, Ukraine my thoughts drifted over our last six weeks of travel when suddenly Phil's voice softly interrupted me.

"Dixey, are you feeling what I'm feeling? In the quiet atmosphere of the bus, I whispered, "Yes, Phil."

Unbeknownst to us, we were entering a flood area fed by a series of rivers. Nadia had not mentioned the rains, nor warned us of taking any precautions. We had no radio to monitor the weather conditions. It turned out that flash flooding spring rains had pounded the Dnieper River Valley which flows through Kiev.

All of a sudden, I felt the rear of the bus fishtailing similar to the motion of a giant shark tail - left, then right, slowly back and forth. One moment the road was in front of me, the very next moment there were only vast expanses of water before me, outlined by my dim headlights.

Would the road take a dip into a valley and take the bus to the bottom?

The responsibility for all the lives aboard had never really weighed so heavily upon me, until that point. It is amazing how much one feels the gravity of a matter in split seconds. I needed to stay sharp on the situation at hand until we made our way through the water. I whispered a prayer. *Oh Lord, what do I do now?*

A memory instantly flashed into my thoughts back from the time I was 17 years old and driving my father's truck and trailer loaded with new Bolen's Lawn Tractors through a wintry snow blizzard from Columbus, Ohio on I-70. When the trailer began sliding to the right side on the ice, I steered to the right. When the trailer slid to the left, I steered ever so slowly back to the left. I made it safely all the way back to Brookville with this method.

I applied this counter steering strategy trying to find traction on the road again. Help came as the gibbous moonlight shone brightly through the broken rain clouds allowing me to see the road beyond my headlights. The silky mud under my wheels felt like we were slowly gliding over packed ice.

I did not apply the brakes or employ the diesel exhaust brake, aware that the sudden loss of traction would spell certain disaster and cast us into the rushing water currents, possibly flipping us over. Easing my foot off the gas pedal slowly, the motor slowed. Gently, the fishtailing stopped, and the road came back into view.

"Hallelujah, we made it!"

Phil whispered, "Good job, Dixey!"

I felt my heart still throbbing in my chest even though the wheels were now on solid road. I relaxed a bit but the respite from disaster only lasted for a few seconds. We lurched again into a water-covered road for a second time. Now a heavy fog was suddenly engulfing us … I could not have seen it coming. With rear wheels fishtailing again, I began counter steering, wondering how long will this stretch last?

Seconds became torturous and it didn't help that there were no reflector signposts anywhere to show me where the road shoulders were. I hoped against hope that my tires would not veer onto the edge of the road at an unseen curve. After some 200 feet of slip sliding, the flooding ended. The road rose out of the lake of water and came into view. *Wow, thank you, Lord!* My heart pounded and I was so relieved the bus wheels found traction with the road again. I applied the exhaust brake, which somehow reminded me of an afterburner on a jet, along with the regular brakes, and stopped as soon as I could.

Would more water inundate the way ahead? Should we drive on farther? Should we wait for daybreak? I needed to corral our convoy drivers and get a consensus, so I signaled them by blinking my running lights three times, then turned on the emergency four-way blinkers.

Nadia asked me "Why have we stopped? We are not allowed to stop the bus anywhere but at the controlled police stops located at major intersections."

I teased Nadia, "If the police come to visit us, maybe they can give us an escort into Kiev. Please explain to them the dangers of the flooded road we just survived."

Discarding any fear, I stepped off the bus and called my drivers together. They told me they started praying for us the moment they saw our bus swaying back and forth across the highway. They had followed along in my tracks, not swerving as much though as their vehicles did not have as high a center of gravity or as long of a wheelbase. Dean Johnson, from the following vehicle said: "We prayed for angels to hold your wheels on the road!" I felt like we had walked on water!

Joining our hands in a circle, we prayed together thanking God for His mercy once again and reminded the Lord to hold His finger on that second radiator repair made at the Soviet border. We'd still need His help if we were to make it to Kiev.

Finally, we discussed whether we should hold up there and sleep inside the bus by the road until morning or go on. The feeling was unanimous, "Let's get through to Kiev since the flooding might get worse if we linger. Most of our group on the bus had slept through the entire saga not realizing the brush with death we narrowly escaped. Fortunately, the Soviet Police did not come. God had been with us.

We resumed our travel to the camping ground reserved for us in Kiev.

Exhausted, I was happy we did not have to erect our tents (another hour's work), as the Intourist Bureau had planned for us to stay in small bungalows. The bureau profited from us by not letting us use our own tents. A Communist regime tries to get all of the hard currency it possibly can.

The overnight lodging was part of our itinerary approved with our visas. We stayed in Kiev for three days for sightseeing, visiting World War II monuments, historic tourist sites, and the city's museums. Our visit was quite informative.

I removed the fractured radiator from the bus by draining it and ratcheting four bolts off and two hose clamps. Nadia arranged for a repair shop to pick it up.

The repair guy laughed when he saw the spark plug sticking out of the radiator, thinking I must really be a dumb American. I laughed with him as I tried to explain with hand signs about the temporary fix.

The following day, the newly welded radiator returned. I reinstalled it and filled it with radiator fluid from our Mercedes truck supply box. I wondered how strong the repair would be. I started the diesel to check for leaks. The old diesel motor turned over at the switch of the key and never once failed to start. I hoped everything would operate again, good as new. As usual, we would trust our future to our Lord.

12

The Unknown

PREPARE FOR A LEAP into the bizarre physical and spiritual worlds of the unknown.

Leaving Kiev, Nadia, our Russian tour guide, did not seem to notice the roughness of our ride. She sat in the passenger seat while I drove. My wife and the other 35 missionaries bumped around in the back seats as the bus trundled over uneven concrete slab roads. *Boom - down, boom – sideways*! We bounced and rocked like a boat tossing in rough seas for the next 300 miles.

In this part of the Eastern Bloc, the sun rises at 4 a.m. and sets at 11:30 p.m., making it a long workday for ordinary folks. We drove past dilapidated homes and bombed-out villages that people have lived in since WWII.

Unlike bus stops in the West, we observed groups of 50 or more people lined up for work on roadsides at 5 a.m. They carried their own rakes, picks and shovels as tractors pulling farm wagons loaded them to go to the massive coop farms. Their sunburned faces were grimacing over the long day ahead of them, appearing as depressed as the scenery surrounding them and wearing outdated, faded clothing, likely leftovers from the 1930s and 40s. It was obvious those citizens living in these parts of the world experienced a dreary existence with no escape nor hope for their future.

Our hearts went out to those impoverished souls. But changing a culture entrenched in socialism takes a lifetime of education and God's omnipotent grace upon the entire nation. The collectivized Soviet Union state-owned farms became impoverished during the Stalin regime under socialistic policies. Some 10 million people died from famine during that time. The grim results remained. After decades, not much had changed.

Alongside town roads we noticed hand-dug wells positioned some 250 meters apart. Fresh water was a priority, even more than food. People came to these wells and gathered buckets of water to take back to their homes. We could do nothing to help them but pray. The rural culture we passed looked like we had driven amongst a people trapped in a time warp, reminiscent of the 1885 Old West era.

Since our journey began early that day, we stopped in a village near Oryol at mid-afternoon. Tired to the bone from hours and hours of travel, we wearily disembarked. Nadia collected our passports and took the necessary vouchers to pay for our rooms in what looked like a bombed-out motel.

Our quarters were another sad story. Had we crossed into Rod Sterling's *Twilight Zone*? The peeling, garish, orange colored wallpaper with fractured spider web-like cracks, turned our stomachs. Toilets and sinks weren't functioning properly and running water was a joke. Julie and I glared at the surroundings and dropped our luggage on the dirty bedroom floor. What next?

She switched on a dusty lamp to dispel the gloomy atmosphere, but the 20-watt light bulb barely lit the room. I plopped down on the bed's sagging mattress, fully dressed, and passed out with Julie by my side, holding hands for comfort.

From a deep sleep, I abruptly awoke gasping for air. Giant hands from an unseen presence clutched my throat and began choking me! Unable to catch my breath, I fought off hysteria, afraid I would die. Some kind of invisible entity hovered above, below, and around me, holding me in its vice. Unable to call out for help, my feet and hands hung limply. Eyes open, I lay in bed terrified with no way to fight back.

As I could make no sounds, in my thoughts I could only muster three words.

"*Jesus, help me*!"

My disembodied assaulter felt like personified evil. It was attacking me with a hatred and violence that only Jesus could stand against, so I kept up my voiceless cries to Him *"Jesus, help me! Jesus save me!"*

After what seemed like hours, I slowly started to feel my lips moving again in relation to my prayer. By now Julie was leaning over me, shaking my shoulders to wake me. This was *not* a nightmare; the attack was real! My lungs starved for air.

I stared up at Julie as she loudly pronounced a prayer for deliverance over me in the name of Jesus. The evil presence started to lose its grip on me and gradually peace began to permeate my suffocation at hearing her passionate words.

Barely whispering, I joined her in prayer for my full deliverance. I then felt this demonic entity loosening its grip from my neck and 'evaporating'.

I sucked in huge gasps of air as if I'd risen to the surface, having just escaped deep, murky waters. Every stitch of my clothing was soaked with sweat and the blanket beneath me was wet through to the bed sheets. Very slowly, I was able to move and speak normally again. "Thank you, Jesus!"

To this day, no evil experience compares to what happened then. Julie saw it was not a mere dream, but something otherworldly; a supernatural force filled with intent, malice, and anger directed specifically at me. Possibly, one of Satan's emissaries sent to thwart the future God had planned for us.

From reading the New Testament, I now understood what the Apostle Paul was saying when he said he fought off beasts. Or what the angel experienced when the prophet Daniel fasted and prayed to Jehovah when the angel was opposed by the Prince of Persia in the heavenlies (I Cor. 15:32; Dan. 10:13). Yet, in both cases, God had delivered them.

I believed God would never forsake or leave me.

As we left our room of horrors, we loaded our luggage back onto the bus. I checked the oil and water level of the radiator to make sure we were good to go for the next 300 miles. This experience with a demonic entity propelled Julie and me to pray over every new location where we stopped to rest on our Soviet journey.

We shared what happened to us with the rest of the group when we gathered together to pray for the next leg of our journey and encouraged them to pray over the future rooms on the rest of our trip. Thankfully, I've never had a reoccurrence of that experience.

Our three months of travels rewarded us with a broader understanding of how religious and non-religious belief systems, i.e. Islam, Catholicism, Atheism and Judaism impact the whole of life for generations. We learned how world views inform and build cultures, people groups and history. We learned to apply Biblical principles to help solve hunger, poverty and illiteracy. We began friendships that remain to this day. We gave the Russian Bibles that made it through the border to interested Russians we met in Moscow.

Our travel for the remainder of the trip was safe. Upon our return to the castle, our training concluded. We farewelled our fellow missionaries who went on to their summer of service phase of training. Julie and I boarded our jet and flew back to the States to prepare for my studies at Miami University - Oxford, Ohio.

13

Learning to Live by Faith

OUR NEXT TWO-AND-A-HALF years at Miami University flew by. Julie worked several different jobs to help cover our living expenses during college and on my last semester's final exam day, she brought forth our first child, Rachael Erin, in May of 1977. In August, I graduated with a Bachelor of Science in Business and my pilot's license after finishing my last classes of integral and differential calculus. I felt my business management major and my minor in international marketing would serve us well to advance the gospel.

We'd kept in touch with our friends, David and Carol Boyd, who continued directing YWAM Germany at Hurlach Castle. After I graduated Miami (of Ohio), David and Carol invited Julie and me to join their staff and be part of the leadership team to oversee the upcoming School of Evangelism (SOE). John Hess, Peter Odewage and I would work under Jim and Judy Orred if we decided to return.

We loved that opportunity but struggled with future plans following my graduation from Miami University. I knew I needed seminary training if I were to become a fully ordained pastor. But to earn a Master's Degree in Divinity would involve another three to four years of full-load classwork. The idea held little attraction in comparison to doing missionary work in Europe.

Higher education might be something I'd revisit in the future.

We remembered the stories of Keith and Marion Warrington's work with YWAM back in Germany when I was in the Army. They'd traveled thousands of miles through the Sahara Desert spreading the gospel. Those tales left an indelible imprint upon our lives since Julie and I were passionate about our faith and changing the world.

The tug of action and adventure in living an uncharted life of faith won over our hearts. I much preferred that over a slow-moving academic setting. As Julie and I prayed, we sensed God calling us back to the YWAM Castle community in Hurlach, Germany. It would become our next phase of trusting God. We also decided to keep supporting our Korean orphan, Bong Kyu Lee, even though we had no idea where the monthly financial support would come from.

We prepared to return to Germany and believed that God would take care of us. My four months of hitchhiking over 5,000 miles back in early 1971 taught me that God provides for every need. I figured if God provided for

Moses and some two million followers wandering 40 years in the desert, He could manage our needs.

YWAM's founder, Loren Cunningham had taught us that where God guides, He provides. When you do the possible, God does the impossible.

With four months left, I worked the night shift at Dayton-Flex in Eaton, Ohio, as a latex glove machine operator. Night work paid time and a half, and weekends, double time. I put in 50-hour weeks to pay off the $6,000 debt from both of our education loans over the previous years. We didn't want to go into missions with debt hanging over our heads. After that, we saved what little we could.

We shared our vision to return to the mission field with friends and our Eaton Presbyterian Church. It wasn't long before we received our first gift check. It came from our interim pastor, Rev. Edwin Woodbury. Julie and I were both shocked and humbled and were filled with such gratitude and affirmation. God seemed to confirm our leading. Pastor Ed drove from Xenia to Eaton to conduct four Sunday worship services each month. He earned a total of $325 monthly from this pastoral retirement work. His gift of $650 (two month's pay) paid for our two one-way flights to Brussels, Belgium and covered the train fare connection to Hurlach. Six-month-old Rachael flew for free. Leaving for Europe with a total savings of $200 in pocket, we trusted that God would provide our monthly income thereafter as each need arose.

Our flight to Brussels went smoothly as did the train ride to Hurlach. Traveling in Europe became second nature after the 6,000-mile Middle East field trip we had made years before. David and Carol greeted us warmly at the Landsberg am Lech train station and shared about the coming YWAM School of Evangelism.

Seeing the castle again took our breath away. It felt like we were home again. Julie and I looked fondly at each other, knowing we'd made the right choice to return.

David carried our bags up to the first floor of the five-floor castle, to settle into our one bedroom, just large enough to also accommodate Rachael in a crib. Bathrooms and showers were a flight of stairs below us.

In January we rejoiced at seeing over 30 students arrive from around the world. Knowing they would become a part of our lives was both challenging and affirming. We all settled into the 1978 SOE schedule of prayer, morning classes, work duties, worship, and evening classes. Weekends were free time.

On Sundays, I drove students to the Augsburg military base for chapel services in the same bus (Katy) I'd driven to Moscow three years earlier.

Our first monthly support began coming from my friend, Jerry Gillespie, whom I had met and prayed with to receive Jesus as his Lord and Savior at the

Middletown branch of Miami University back in August of 1975. He pledged to send us $50 a month. Jerry was the first and only one to financially support us in our early missionary days, regularly sending us money during the three years we were in Germany with YWAM. Our friendship has endured to this day.

The ideal would have been to have several people committing a monthly pledge to support us or a church supporting us through their missionary giving program. We discovered that many missionaries had full monthly support from their friends and churches. We did not have a mission focused church to help us, but God still came through each month with what we needed.

Occasionally, a man named Sparky Oldfather sent us a check through the Eaton Presbyterian Church. I'll never forget what Sparky said one Easter morning following a senior Sunday School class on the atonement of Christ I taught while attending Miami University. With tears streaming down his face, he said: "Dixey, today, for the first time in my life, I really understand why Jesus had to die for my sins. Can you show me how to receive Jesus into my life like you spoke about?"

I had the solemn privilege of leading Sparky to Christ back then. The scripture in II Corinthians 5:17 (NIV) comes to mind. "Therefore, if anyone is in Christ, he is a new creation; the old has gone, the new has come!"

Even at the age of 80, Sparky became a new creation! Because of his love for Jesus, he wanted to support us. Also, my brother, Bruce also a missionary, occasionally sent us support.

Finances usually came just as we needed it. Faith grows when you actually experience God providing your needs each month. This may sound like a cockamamie way to live, but it always came together.

An unexpected source of $60 monthly income came from the German government called "Kindergeld" (children's money). Every person living in Germany with a child received government child welfare support, even foreign missionaries. What a surprise! We had extra to spend for a case of Coke each month and we could afford Rachael's 'Luvs' brand of baby diapers.

For the next three months, our roster of teachers was an astonishing array of young Christian leaders with different ministries and backgrounds. Five of my favorites were Derek Prince from the UK; Loren Cunningham, YWAM's founder; and Erlo Steggen, a South African revival preacher. We learned to hear God's voice through praying daily in our groups during the SOE and three-month field trip. David and Carol Boyd also taught us about relationships, faith and community that they had learned on their faith journey.

Their instructions prepared us for the most exciting vision yet to come. Trusting God for finances expanded to trusting God for others' needs as well.

14

A Cruise Ship for World Missions

AFTER LOREN CUNNINGHAM founded YWAM in Le Chalet-a-Gobet in Lausanne, Switzerland and established multiple YWAM bases in Germany, England, France, Switzerland, Austria, Holland, Spain and Greece, he named Don Stephens as YWAM Director over Europe and Africa.

Forming a youthful evangelical group begins with young people yearning to share their Christian faith on a shoestring budget, believing in a big God who cares about them and taking up the cross and following Jesus. After years of training and discipleship in Switzerland, Loren and his wife, Darlene moved to Hawaii to establish a missionary base which eventually grew into University of the Nations on Kona Island.

When living among men and women who eat, sleep, think, work, breathe and dream on a faith level echelons above your own, opportunities to grow in Christ abound. Their life discipline is great inspiration for growing your own personal faith. Like everything else in life, faith is developed through practice.

Faith in God is never mastered but can be stretched. Building a strong faith is similar to an athlete exercising his or her muscles through training. Their goal involves vigilance to sustain a routine of diet and exercise alongside the right training programs. Some have 'faith muscles' akin to Arnold Schwarzenegger, a winner of Mr. Universe seven times. But just dreaming of success did not strengthen his muscles. In 1 Corinthians 12: 4-13, the Apostle Paul shares his insight into the gifts of the Holy Spirit. Gifts of faith, miracles, and healing are but a few of the benefits gifted by God for the building up the church. Work, discipline, sacrifice, study, prayer, commitment and passion are part of the formula.

Vigilant Christians who practice faith achieve more in life. Certain men and women have a larger affinity and capacity for achieving faith. They are born with a gift of 'spiritual prowess' – an affinity for seeing situations before they exist. They hear God's voice, believe and speak their visions into existence.

That is what 'living by faith' can do for believers! That's what YWAM teaches people during their discipleship training school (DTS).

During the 1978 SOE lecture, Don Stephens offered a challenge to each of the YWAM European base leaders. We were to pray and ask God to provide special financial support to purchase an 11,000 ton, 520 foot ship. The appeal included asking each base to pledge a monthly 'faith promise' amount to get a humanitarian ship ministry vision afloat and sail the seas. The 1953 ship, M/V Victoria was mothballed and docked in Venice, Italy.

God led Julie and me to trust for this, asking God to put a number in our minds that He wanted to release through us for this ministry. After praying we finally agreed on $1,000 to give for the ship (in addition to our normal monthly living expenses). This financial goal seemed impossible; yet we wanted to trust God.

We had no bank account or idea of how much prayer it would take for the goal to be met. We would sacrifice all other non-essential purchases until the full $1,000 arrived, e.g., we gave up our monthly ration of a case of Coke and returned to washing cloth diapers. We made sure to tell no one else of our faith promise but God. We trusted God for additional income in excess of our needs of the regular $50 a month Jerry Gillespie committed to us. Other gifts flowed in from unfamiliar people and places. We committed every additional penny received to the ship pledge.

Over a period of four months, one third of the entire amount came from an Army Captain who attended a military retreat in Vilseck where I had spoken on *Knowing God*. The full balance arrived in $25, $50, and $100 increments over that same time period. That's three times the amount we had ever received. It's special because we told no one else about this special project. Receiving the full $1,000 for the ship was a miracle to us! That challenge really caused our faith to grow stronger.

At the end of our three-month SOE, our 30 students plus 12 others who flew in from the Bozeman, Montana YWAM base boarded a train for Venice to join with 300+ others at Camping Jolly for launching the new ship ministry.

15

Moses, Our Mentor

GOD'S PROPHET MOSES, the central character in the Book of Exodus, led the Children of Israel out of Egypt on a long journey to the Promised Land. He trusted that *Jehovah Jireh* (the God who provides) would supply the needs of over two million men, women, and children for however long it took.

We believed that during our first six weeks in Venice, Italy we would purchase a ship, the M/V Victoria. It was mothballed in a shipyard near Camping Jolly. Then, we would sail it to the site of the 1978 FIFA World Cup Soccer Games in June to Argentina. There, we would witness the love of God to world travelers. Following the Soccer Games, we planned on launching the ship into a fulltime missionary training, humanitarian aid and medical ship that would sail into the ports of Africa to assist the needy.

However, we discovered rather soon that visions do not always pan out as initially planned. I doubt if Moses set out with a 40-year plan in mind, he probably planned 6 months to a year at most. Our six-week preparation stage turned into a lingering four months and beyond.

Nationwide strikes in Italy crippled our preparations. Unfortunately, only a few sailors showed up. The certification for flagging the ship and inspections were delayed. Many needed repairs were discovered as we inspected deeper into the bowels the ship. Hopes and dreams of the gathered three hundred faithful believers sleeping in tents and waiting for departure hung in the balance. Some had spent their last dime to be part of this new ship vision.

Would these unexpected events result in a colossal fiasco of well-meaning but misguided youth? Time would tell. In our instant-success seeking world and high tech instant-global communication systems, we've become mesmerized and hypnotized by speed so much, that we've forgotten that growth takes time.

A child falls down how many times before learning to walk? A spiritual child also follows a similar pattern. And then, it's still a long way to adulthood. Things of the Spirit are not instant like so many things that we have immediately available in the grocery store.

Just a cursory reading of Moses' trials in the book of Exodus give insight to the challenges and trials you will face when you set your heart to obey God at any cost. Space does not suffice here to elucidate; we learned a major principle: spiritual growth happens over the long run.

* * *

The Fund proposal made to a specific individual that our leaders prepared to procure financing for the $1 million purchase price fell through. After the marine survey, the many repairs needed to flag the ship would demand at least two years of drydock, maintenance and rebuilding. Just to fill the light grade and heavy grade crude oil tanks would cost well over $200,000 and we would need well over 100 trained able-bodied seamen just to operate the vessel. We didn't even have a Captain!

* * *

There were good signs though. As bookkeeper for the entire group, I had many insights into the internal affairs of financing. After our first six weeks, we purchased the ship with 10% down and took a $900,000 loan from the Italiano Credito. The leadership changed the name M/V Victoria to M/V Anastasis, meaning *Resurrection*, in Greek.

While the Anastasis ship received repairs, the leaders gathered the 300+ YWAMers at Camping Jolly and channeled our focus to immediate outreaches locally and European wide.

Our teams spread out across the countries of Spain, Italy, Yugoslavia, Israel, Turkey, Malta and France fanning the flames of the gospel by preaching in smaller groups on the streets and in churches, Catholic and Protestant alike. Many responded to our preaching on the streets and yielded their lives to Christ. A contingent of our YWAMers later flew to the global outreach at the World Cup Games in Argentina and new YWAM bases grew out of the new contacts that came from the re-structuring.

When we began to realize that this would take much longer than planned. Don had Mark Spengler, our accountant, order tugboats to tug the *Anastasis* to a port in Greece to finish the refit because of the many shipyard strikes that could postpone the refit schedule indefinitely.

Many of our missionaries went to Greece to join the long-term refit. The remaining missionaries returned to our bases throughout Europe to continue with our summer of service outreaches. You will see more of the exciting story of the *Anastasis* ministry in a later chapter.

16

If God can use Dr. Prince, will He also use Me?

JULIE AND I CONTINUED TO learn lessons on exercising our faith while attending The School of Evangelism (SOE) classes. The faith walks of other missionaries personally impacted us and created monumental changes in our own lifestyles.

In 1979, Dr. Derek Prince, a former Chair of the Philosophy Department at Cambridge University, England, taught in our SOE for one week. I admired his tall stature, deep baritone voice with a British accent, and his vast intellectual ability to infuse a powerful punch into every line. I recall this one:

"If God is willing to use another person to perform healing, then God, who is no respecter of persons, may also be willing to use other believers in the same manner."

One evening, Dr. Prince taught us how to release the supernatural power of God into our lives. A particular student (whom I shall call "Diane") drew my attention. She leaned forward, seeming to inhale every detail of his teaching on God's healing power. I saw tears form, lecture after lecture, while taking meticulous notes.

He said if we apply the same spiritual disciplines and principles he had, we would be able to heal others, too.

"Be healed in Jesus' name!" are powerful words in the hands of people who trust God for miracles. *Would I be able to heal, too?*

He also demonstrated God's power, sharing how he'd laid hands on people, and on many occasions, they'd received instantaneous healings. He then, invited anyone who desired to be healed to come for prayer.

Diane stepped forward and sat down in a chair in front of the podium, as instructed, expressing her desire to be healed from the affliction of polio. Wearing foot and leg braces to help correct her early childhood affliction, she eventually learned to walk without them with the aid of a one-inch lift built into the heel of one shoe. She had courageous faith to become everything God intended for her.

"May I take your shoes off?" he asked her. "That way, when God heals you, everyone can see God doing the healing. I am not the healer; the Lord Jesus Christ is. My only job is to pray, believe, and demonstrate my faith to release God's power. Healing is like sticking an electric plug into a wall socket. I am the connection link between you and God who has the power to heal. Do you understand that, Diane?"

She said, "Yes."

We were all excited over the idea of Diane being healed, - leaning forward in our seats to get a better view.

Dr. Prince proclaimed, "Diane, in the name of Jesus, I command you to be healed." He bent down on his knees directly in front of her, held her heels in his hands and compared the length of her legs. One was an inch shorter than the other.

I was afraid she might not be healed, and her faith would be damaged. Confidently, he then addressed the very questions on my mind, as if he'd heard me say them aloud.

"Some of you are thinking what if God does not heal her? I want to say again that I am not the healer. God is! My only job in this process is to pray. The rest is up to God." Then Dr. Prince began thanking God for Diane's healing.

"I thank you God that you hear me now and that you are healing Diane as I speak. I thank you for healing her in the name of your son, Jesus Christ."

He paused while we all held our breath.

"Look!" he exclaimed. "There it is! Her leg is stretching out!"

Incredibly, we watched in awe as Diane's shorter leg stretched out to the same length as her other one. Over a short period of nearly two minutes her legs were the same length. As Diane's husband of 10 years watched the healing process, his eyes filled with tears. As she stood to walk without her shoes, we were astounded to see her walking perfectly. I savored the smile on Derek's face and the glorious reward of Diane's faith. You can only imagine how our faith in God was increased after witnessing so powerful a miracle; praising God through tears of joy.

Something was different about how Derek prayed. He *expected* God to do what he asked. I went to bed that night praying, *'God, will you use me to do what you did through Derek?'* His teaching and example had so propelled my faith that I began asking God to use me in the same way.

However, I battled the fear of failure. The voice of fear asked me, *'What if you pray, and God doesn't do anything? What if you say, 'be healed' and nothing happens?'* Doubting questions bombarded my mind. I needed greater faith in myself, God's promises and His ability. From then on, I prayed more specifically that God would release His healing power through me.

I spent three months studying and praying over every healing moment in the life of Christ as written in the gospels. I outlined each healing, action and words, and their resulting impact. *Will You, God, consider using me to do what Derek did?*

I finally arrived at thinking no matter whether or not God healed the person I prayed for, I would still trust Him, believing in His power regardless of mindset or fearful feelings.

The time would soon come when I confronted my fears and confessed my faith.

17

My Second Healing Miracle

KEITH WARRINGTON, OUR director for Jugend Mit einer Mission (JMEM is the German acronym for YWAM), asked me if I would pray about taking a team to Bergen, Germany, to conduct a discipleship training weekend for a Youth Ski Retreat in the Alps. Since I loved working with youth and relished the idea of snow skiing, teaching and worship, I could not imagine a more enjoyable weekend.

The offer felt more like a reward. This would be the first retreat I would lead in a totally German context. Since German youth are required to take six years of English in school, most would understand me, but we took an interpreter with us, just to cover all the bases.

Keith told me there was already a strong believing group of about 35 Christian teenagers that *Frau (Mrs.) Walter* had mentored for several years. Her husband of 50 years pastored a Lutheran church near Salzburg, Austria.

I would also be taking Roy Edwards along with us, a wonderful worship leader who had great rapport with young people. Another gifted young leader, Frank, would be my translator. After several days of intense praying, the Holy Spirit confirmed I should lead this team, so I gave Keith the thumbs up.

Julie would accompany me, as well as Rachael, our two-year-old daughter. We'd depart for Bergen in approximately three weeks.

Our team consisting of Roy, Frank, Julie and I met on several occasions prior to leaving, praying and putting together a schedule for the activities during the mission weekend. We chose the subject matter and who would teach each of the six sessions. Sunday morning would be devoted to worship, teaching, communion and for commissioning.

The snow-covered Bavarian chalets dotted the alpine foothills of Bergen as we exited the Munich-Salzburg autobahn. Great excitement and expectation filled the exuberant youth who came out to greet us. It reminded me of the retreats I attended during my college days. Everyone in our group sensed the palpable presence of God. With so much prayer and preparation, we believed something wonderful was going to happen during our meetings. Nothing compares to the presence of the Holy Spirit as God welcomes believers who are sensitive to His powerful work of grace.

Upon arrival, we were delighted to meet with Frau Walter, a dignified gray-haired lady about 76 years old, full of joyous compassion, spiritual strength, and enthusiasm for youth. She appeared much younger and possessed a rare spiritual beauty, seasoned with laughter and a gracious smile.

The following morning after our Thursday evening teaching session, we donned our ski suits and gear. The double chair ski lift was right outside our back door. We needed only to use the herringbone ski technique to climb up to the lift and begin our ascent up the mountain. Everyone was excited.

Frau Walter was right behind me on her skis! I asked her, "Isn't this a little bit demanding for you?" She smiled and said, "I have been skiing since I was five, and if God lets me, I'll ski until I am 90!" She possessed an eager and winsome spirit.

As we rode the chair lift together, she told me of her terrible skiing fall seven years before. The doctor had patched up her broken hip and one of her legs with pins, but that injury had not stopped her from skiing. After about three months in a cast, nine months on crutches, she once again returned to the ski slopes.

At times, the pain in her back became quite severe, so she took medication. She never slept past four o'clock in the morning due to pain that woke her. But that didn't matter; she used the time to pray.

I noticed when I first met Frau Walter that she had a slight limp. "But" she proclaimed with a sparkle in her eyes, "I will never let pain stop me from skiing with my young people!" It was apparent Frau Walter's youth loved her, often checking on her during our skiing outings. At first, I was reluctant to ski too fast, not wanting to overwhelm her. However, she skied right past me, blazing down the slope – I couldn't keep up!

The retreat went beautifully as planned. The youth were dedicated and hungry to know God better. Their zealous pursuit of learning the Word of God set them apart from all groups I'd ever been with. These young people were incredible.

By Sunday morning, our team sensed that God wanted us to revise our schedule. Instead of a commissioning service, we would conduct a 'blessing service' to speak words of encouragement or prophecy over each person who came forward for prayer.

Roy was especially sensing this so I asked him if he would lead the meeting and I would follow. We began laying our hands upon the shoulders and heads of each young person. Several others came forward to support and pray with their friends.

The Holy Spirit would speak a 'word' or show an 'image' in our minds, revealing to us how to speak wisdom over each person. As we testified to what God had shown us through thoughts and visuals, the students marveled. They were aware of their friends' interests, strengths and desires, and were amazed how accurately the words from God fit each one exactly—from strangers whom they'd never met before.

In one instance, God revealed to me that one particular young woman would become a missionary and a great teacher. Others in the group knew she had a gift of teaching and that she had been sharing with them over the last couple of years about how she wanted to become a missionary. The Spirit had given us these insights through the 'gift of knowledge.' (I Corinthians 12:8)

That day, after all of the students had received a 'word', Frau Walter came up to the front and asked for prayer. As I placed my hands upon her, the Lord spoke to me, *"Dixey, I want you to pray for her to be healed from her skiing injury she told you about."* God's voice was decisive and clear.

Patiently, she peered at me for a moment, so I asked her, "Frau Walter, what would you like from the Lord?"

"Dixey, the Lord has already told you what I would like from the Lord." That settled the question.

Since this was my first attempt to pray for someone in public to be healed in the manner Derek Prince had demonstrated, I did not want to look foolish if nothing happened. So, I asked the youth to remain seated in the meeting room and pray, while our team went into a separate room to pray with Frau Walter to receive healing. Most of them had witnessed her skiing accident years before. They would stay and pray.

Present with us that day were three young German men whom Frau Walter had discipled through their teens and into adulthood. They were seminary students attending Tuebingen University, studying to become Lutheran ministers. I invited them to pray with us in the other room.

I faced my fears and prayed, *Lord, I believe, help my unbelief.* Both excited and believing, yet still a little doubtful, I was confident in God's power to heal. *But would He really use me to do it?* The moment had arrived. It's now or never.

I had Frau Walter sit in a chair and asked her seminary students to stand behind and lay hands upon her. It was going to take all of our faith together to perform a miracle of healing. They did not know what was about to happen, nor had they ever seen someone do this before; neither had they heard of Derek Prince.

I asked Frau Walter if I could take off her shoes. Holding her heels in the palms of my hands I compared the length of her legs.

"You have a leg nearly a half inch shorter than the other one." The seminary students saw the difference in the length of her legs; they agreed it was true.

I spoke directly to her left leg as if it had ears to hear me. "Left leg, in the name of Jesus, I command you to grow out." I paused … nothing happened. Closing my eyes, I visualized her leg growing out; then opening my eyes … still nothing had happened.

The seminary students and my team watched and kept praying in whispers. I began to question if I was doing the right thing by putting myself into this precarious situation. I quietly said to God, *Lord, I really need you to hear my prayer.*

I repeated, "Left leg, I command you to grow out and be healed, in the name of Jesus." *Again – no change. Lord, why have I put myself into this position? If you do not do something, I will look like a fool. The reputation of YWAM will be damaged and I will bring discredit upon your name. I really need you to heal Frau Walter, Lord."*

Then, I thought, *I am going to try this one more time and Lord, if you don't heal her now, I don't know if I will ever have the courage to try this healing thing again.* I boldly proclaimed "Left leg! In the name of Jesus Christ, I command you to grow out as far as the other leg!"

Instantly, Frau Walter's leg shot out and lengthened.

Trembling, she said, "I just felt a jolt of electricity going through my entire body. God has touched me!"

The three Tuebingen seminary students examined the alignment of her feet. They were perfectly equal in length. They could not believe what had just happened and they began shouting, "We have seen a miracle! God has healed Frau Walter!"

Excited, they ran down the hallway toward where the youth were gathered and praying. "We have seen a miracle happen right in front of our eyes – Frau Walter is healed! God has healed her!"

Roy, Frank, and I walked with Frau Walter back into the room where the students were dancing, shouting, and running up to hug her. Full of thankfulness she told them all, "The pain is gone! It's gone! It's gone! Jesus touched me – I am whole!" Everyone was elated. Roy picked up the guitar and led the group in singing, "The Joy of the Lord is My Strength."

Frau Walter went over to the staircase and said, "I want you all to see this!" She ran up and down the stairs without hesitation and without pain. Then she walked across the room without the limp I had noticed on the first day. She let out a hoop and a holler saying "*Preiset den Herrn*!" (Praise the Lord!)

Following the weekend when Frau Walter was healed, our team returned to Hurlach Castle, rejoicing in the wonderful grace of God. I had learned, *If God will use Dr. Prince, He will use me, too.*

* * *

Two months later, as I walked down a street in Munich to attend a church service where Derek Prince was speaking, I heard someone yelling from across the street. A lady wearing a heavy winter coat and shawl waved her hands at me. There was a much taller young man beside her. *Did I know her?* She shouted again and ran across the street toward me. Turning to the younger gentleman, she said: "It's him, it's Dixey, it's Dixey! He's the one." I recognized Frau Walter as she got closer. She hugged me as her companion caught up with her and shook my hand.

"So, mother," he said to her, "this is Dixey, the man whom God used to heal you at the youth retreat, the one you have been telling me about?" She answered, "Yes, he is the one. Dixey obeyed God, and I will be forever grateful!"

We walked into the Derek Prince church conference and sat together through the service. *Thank you, Lord for your faithfulness! Your mercies are new every morning.*

I was so grateful to God for allowing me to help someone who desperately needed his touch. Asking Frau Walter if any pain had returned and if she was sleeping all night now, she said, "I feel like I did when I was a teenager. I have more energy now than ever. The pain has not returned and I sleep all night!"

Jesus spoke in Luke 4 about *the anointing.* I sensed something within me was released that day two months earlier when things shifted from simply preaching and teaching into the healing streams of believing for the supernatural through faith. It's difficult to describe. My extended times of seeking God, intense personal prayers, Bible study and reflection, followed by action, resulted in a life-changing power that had made another person's walk through this life less painful, more enjoyable, and life-transforming. I was so grateful that God put His desire in my heart.

18

Healing and Attempting Deliverance

THE MANIFESTATION OF GOD'S gracious healing presence always amazes me. The very fact that God chose me to disburse His redemptive healing upon the sick and injured extols His magnificence. I was very humbled when God chose to use me to touch and heal another person. Would He choose to do it again?

When the leaders of a certain Christian group in Germany asked me if I believed it was possible for a woman afflicted with a demon to be set free, I replied, "Definitely." I did not foresee the question that followed. When they asked if I believed God would use me to do it, I said, "Let me fast and pray and get back to you."

It's my belief that God always wants to move believers to a higher level of faith. I had limited experience with exorcism. The upcoming retreat would change my perception of ministry for a lifetime. I reasoned that if Jesus delivered people from evil back in His day … He can do it again today.

After 19 days of progressive fasting (one meal a day the first week, two meals a day the second week and three meals a day for most of the third week), God gave me the confidence that He would deliver the demon-afflicted woman in this group. I called the leader and told him, "Yes, I believe God will use me to help this lady."

We arranged a retreat with their group and set a date. This would be my first experience addressing an evil entity in a public setting.

From reading the scriptures, I knew that I had no control over the consequences when dealing with demons. Sometimes there are more than one demon. Even the disciples failed at times and needed Jesus to help them. Mary Magdalene had seven demons before Jesus met her; the Gadarene demoniac had a thousand.

I did not have the luxury of walking beside Jesus and learning by experience from Him as the 12 disciples did. But I trusted in the presence of the Holy Spirit, the power of the name of Jesus, and the holy Word of God.

When people in America or civilized countries hear the words 'demon possessed,' they generally think of the movie, *The Exorcist.* I find that Hollywood films are a poor comparison to the actual experience. The subject of 'occult' and 'dark forces' are usually met with ridicule in our modern age. Notions of actually performing an exorcism are generally scorned and laughed at. But when I did a close study of Biblical scriptures, they revealed that Jesus treated demon possession with compassion, prayer, and overpowering authority. Our Lord never perceived demonic activity as anything but what it really was, dealing with a lesser abhorrent evil messenger of Satan.

Satan is devoid of truth, love, light and righteousness. Jesus always set people free even when the local villagers were disturbed by it. Dr. Derek Prince has noted that the Greek word used in the King James Bible does not actually mean possession.

Demonesthesae means 'demons dwell with a person, or a person lives with demons.' The actual word 'possession' does not exist in *Koine Greek* in the Bible in any texts where exorcisms occur. The idea that a person is 'possessed' by a demon is a mistranslation in the King James version. The fact is that the demon does have influence over some portion of a human being, but only in a particular area.

On the appointed day, I went with my wife, Julie, daughter Rachael and my translator, Astrid Breckwoldt. My hopes were high for an outpouring of God's mercy and power. Some 30 members of this Bible study group had gathered for the weekend in a quaint alpine chalet guesthouse. We met the leaders and sat down with them for a modest German cuisine together, then gathered in the conference room for worship, praise and teaching. After the service, I invited folks to come forward for prayer.

Sometimes, you can sense the presence of depression and evil. Everyone in the group knew Helga and the depression she lived under. They had prayed for her for years and no one had been able to help her. She had seen countless doctors, psychiatrists, psychologists and therapists, only to come away with an empty bank account. She tried seances, mediums and witches – all to no avail.

Would God do what no human could? Would He lift her out of the stupor of depression? We all waited with anticipation to see what would happen.

On the first evening a lady (I will call "Helga") lined up at the very front of the prayer line. God's Spirit spoke to me. '*Have her sit down and wait; pray for the others first.*'

Not understanding why God said that, I kindly asked Helga to sit down and allow others to come before her. I had never seen eyes like hers; they were clouded over with a thin gray substance. *How could she see to walk?*

The next person in line was Gertrude, a classical piano teacher who had been through a horrific experience 11 months previously. While crossing a street, she failed to see a car that had been parked, begin rolling downhill, picking up speed and heading toward her.

She'd screamed in tremendous pain as the driverless car pinned her hips under the bumper and on to the ground, dragging her along. At the hospital

ER, the doctors mended her fractured hips in three places. But in addition to this trauma, as a grandmother of three, she'd just buried her daughter one month earlier. She died from cancer and there was no father in the picture. Gertrude adopted all three of her grandchildren.

The woman's pain was so great, her bed had to be moved to the main floor of her home since she could no longer climb stairs. I believed I should pray for her healing. So, I asked her to sit down in the same manner as Dr. Prince had demonstrated to us.

In a step of faith, I exclaimed to everyone in the room, "Gertrude will be healed because Jesus Christ is alive and is risen from the dead."

I asked Gertrude, "Is there anything you cannot do?

"I cannot raise my hands above my shoulders."

"Anything else?"

"I cannot bend and stretch my hands below my knees."

"It's too painful to go up and down the stairs."

"Would you remove your shoes?"

She did.

I pulled a chair in front of the group and had her sit in the chair. I kneeled down and held both of her feet straight out so everyone could see the difference in the length of her legs. If they grew, it would indicate that God had healed her hips, her legs and realigned her back. I quietly prayed, then spoke aloud, "I command these legs to be healed in the name of Jesus Christ!"

We all waited and watched. Within seconds, both legs began to move and twitch. Gasps and shouts came from the crowd. Gertrude's shorter leg and longer leg *both* grew forward, till finally the shorter leg caught up to the same length as the longer. Her pain instantly subsided. She stood up and put both hands high into the air. She bent over and touched the floor at my request.

"Do you want to try the stairs?"

Praising Jesus, she ran through the doorway and up and down the stairs.

"No pain, no pain, Jesus healed me, no pain!" Her limp disappeared. The group cheered seeing her joy and total healing. The room filled with songs of praise. The group leader suggested we take up an offering and buy Gertrude a new pair of shoes without the medical lift attached to the heel. I was relieved and thrilled. The tension of believing for the impossible once again had been swallowed up in gratitude to God.

Our collective faith increased and three more people lined up for prayer. God brought victory and healing for them too. When no one else came forward, I motioned for Helga to come forward again to receive her deliverance. The faith-packed anticipation of the crowd was high for Helga's deliverance. They were praying intently.

I spent the next 15 minutes instructing Helga and the group on the process and principles of deliverance. Then I turned to Helga. I led Helga in a prayer of repentance of sin and renunciation of Satan and all of his ways. I bound the powers of Satan and loosed her from his bondage. I looked in her eyes intently and commanded: "Demon, in the name of Jesus, I command you, come out."

Nothing happened. I sensed the demon's presence, but it resisted departing. After much time of deliberate prayer and imploring the demon to leave, I interceded for greater wisdom in knowing how to deal with this difficult stronghold. I was physically growing tired by then and asked the group if we could retire and appeal to God for the answers in the morning. The leaders agreed. We closed with prayer for protection through the night.

19

Deliverance to the Captives

"The Spirit of the Lord is upon me, because he hath anointed me to preach the gospel to the poor; he hath sent me to heal the brokenhearted, to preach deliverance to the captives, and recovering of sight to the blind, to set at liberty them that are bruised." Luke 4:18 (KJV)

SPECIAL NOTE : I feel compelled to share that the Christian church has, for the most part, through the centuries, taught that we are to do exactly what Jesus did, and be 'little Christs' living after His example. "Do," and "Be." Yet, when the subject of demons comes up, church leaders of many mainline denominations have cast a doubting shadow upon anyone who gives credence to the concept that demons exist.

In the face of all evidence that Jesus took the idea and reality of demons as a matter of fact, the church assumes demons were an accommodation by Jesus to the superstitions of the times; that Jesus, Himself, was above such beliefs.

However, the evidence is clear that Jesus manifested some of His greatest healings to those afflicted with demons. I believe that demons cause 'broken-heartedness' and 'bondage.' If people are troubled by such entities, Christians are to follow our Lord's example to set them free, just as Jesus and His disciples did. Jesus acted from humility, compassion, understanding, patience and love in every circumstance where He confronted evil dominating a child or an adult's life. That's what we (His Church) are called to. Should we not also bring freedom to the captives? In the Greek, the word *Ekklesia* is translated "Church." It means "the called-out ones"; that's us!

MY FIRST ATTEMPT TO deliver Helga from the evil spirit had failed. I did not witness God's power release to heal her at all. *Now what do I do, Lord? Why did the other marvelous healings occur, but not Helga's? She's the one I came here for.* There are three instances in Scripture where demons resisted: the Gadarene demoniac who toyed with Jesus, Luke 8:26-39. The disciples failed and asked Jesus to help, Mark 9:14-29. And, the eight Jewish exorcists who failed miserably in Acts 19:15-17.

The experience of spiritual warfare with a defiant resistant demon in a public setting of total strangers had absolutely worn me out. I recalled Ephesians 6:10, 11 (NIV) *"Finally, be strong in the Lord and in his mighty power. Put on the full armor of God, so that you can take your stand against the devil's schemes."* Great advice but, perhaps my 19 days of prayer and fasting were not sufficient. I had to know. Disappointment drove me deeper in prayer. After midnight, I fell asleep praying for God's wisdom and guidance.

Lord, you told me you would heal her!

Five a.m. Morning, ~ a new day!

Perplexed, but not defeated the night before, I knew that God promised me Helga's deliverance. I felt the Holy Spirit telling me to start taking notes. For half an hour the Holy Spirit dictated a number of principles to apply when conducting an exorcism. Perhaps they were specific to this particular person and situation.

I will not detail them at this point, but after the Holy Spirit revealed this teaching to me, I understood why Helga did not receive deliverance.

I met with the group after breakfast and taught them what I had learned regarding the ministry of deliverance. I quoted scriptures the Holy Spirit gave me. It was necessary to totally depend on the Holy Spirit's leadership during a healing session.

There are no set formulas for how individuals with different problems experienced deliverance. The Holy Spirit had instructed me to tell Helga to cease all medications and attend all teaching sessions during the weekend retreat.

I sensed that conducting deliverance without giving extensive training regarding the authority given to each believer through Christ is futile. We all needed to understand that the power of healing is in Jesus' blood and the deliverer's place is one of intercession, teaching, fasting, and vigilance to persist for success.

I also told the group I would not pray for Helga in front of the group. My German interpreter, Astrid, would be with me in a private room with Helga, and we would do extensive counseling and inquiry prior to the next exorcism attempt.

Setbacks and hurdles are not failures.

When the time came for me to meet with Helga after Sunday lunch, everyone else would gather for prayer in a separate room. Helga's husband would remain with the prayer group while Astrid and I met with her in a second-floor room in the hotel.

Her eyes were clouded over as before. She spoke in a brief, fragmented, forced monotone and her whole demeanor bespoke depression. Her colorless personality was dominated by an evil presence that had tormented her for over 20 years.

As the Holy Spirit prompted, I pursued the questions that would clarify our understanding of how this evil presence had taken over her life.

Helga was Catholic but had never read the Bible. She had attended seances and had sought out mediums (forbidden by the Bible). She had no clear understanding of Jesus' death and its impact on the forgiveness of her sins, or that her confession of sin and forgiveness must be personally appropriated.

When asked about her family genealogy, she shared how her father and his three brothers had all committed suicide. Helga's grandfather had also committed suicide.

No wonder familiar spirits visited her. She'd been surrounded by death most of her life and constantly asked "When are you going to commit suicide?"

We counseled Helga through her problems and prayed together.

After leading Helga to confess her sins and repent of them, she invited Christ to come into her life. At that moment, she received eternal life. I then led her to confess, repent, and denounce any association with consulting mediums and witchcraft since it was spiritual adultery forbidden by God. I pressed deeper and addressed the evil spirit directly. I could not see the demon but I could sense its presence.

I knew it was watching me through Helga's eyes.

The demon constricted her vocal cords so she could not say the name of Jesus. I demanded, "*Ich befelle dich Boesse Geist, Im namen Jesu Christi, herauskommen!*" Which means "I command you, evil spirit, in the name of Jesus Christ, come out!"

Helga's body cringed as the evil spirit disregarded my command and ignored me.

I doubled down and declared that Helga's soul belonged to Jesus now, and that the spirit had no entitlement over her any longer. She'd been cleansed by the blood of Jesus, and the spirit was no longer welcome and must submit to my commands according to the Word of God. Still, the spirit resisted. Again, I commanded it to leave.

Still, no reaction. Then I pressed in and said, "Tell me your name, evil spirit, tell me your name, I command you in the name of Jesus!"

In a split second, something punched Helga on the back with the force of horse's hooves. Her upper body flew forward faster than humanly possible and screams of demons, as if burning in hell, flowed from her mouth like a gushing fire hydrant.

Helga's body stayed bent forward over her knees as the loud screaming rage continued beyond one's normal ability to breathe. I looked at Astrid.

She said "What do we do now?" I said, "I don't know, just wait, I guess."

Shrieks and screams of what sounded like male and female-like voices filled the room and continued for what seemed like minutes. (Acts 8:4 in the Bible mentions how impure spirits shriek when forced to leave people.)

The sound of loud footsteps rushing up the main hotel stairs could be heard. Soon, people from the group gathered outside our closed door. They'd been praying for us for the past two hours. They had heard the screaming.

All of a sudden, the screaming stopped. Total silence. We sat and waited patiently. Still bent forward at the waist, Helga whispered in a sweet soft melodious voice, "Can I get up now?" We were hopeful.

"Certainly," I responded.

"Did I hear someone screaming?" she asked us in her newly restored voice.

Helga's beautiful crystal-clear blue eyes were filled with tears and love. The cloudy film over her eyes had disappeared. Pure elation filled the room. Helga was radiant

Then she said, "It's gone, it's gone! Look, I can hold my shoulders up! Something like eagle talons have pressed my shoulders down together for years like a straight-jacket. It's gone! I'm free! I'm free!" She moved her shoulders up and down, forward and backward, jubilantly shouting and celebrating her freedom.

We prayed for her to be filled with the Holy Spirit and welcomed her husband and friends into the room. Seeing Helga shocked them. They saw a new Helga who now had a huge smile and praised Jesus. She'd become a new creation.

A year later, we met the group again, Helga had become a strong radiant Christian and a powerful prayer warrior.

I recently contacted Astrid Breckwoldt in South Africa through her Facebook page. She said she'd never forgotten that most miraculous weekend when Helga was delivered from evil spirits.

20

The Gift of a VW Van

JULIE AND I HAD PRAYED for over eight months to get a vehicle since we had no extra money to buy one. Unexpectedly, in September 1978, I heard "*Wilfried Bially for Dixey Behnken, am Telefon* (on the telephone*)*," over the castle intercom speaker from the reception desk. I made my way from our bedroom on the fourth-floor staircase under the slate-domed spires and stepped down the main spiral staircase of castle to the phone.

"Wilfried, hey, good to hear from you!" We'd met seven years earlier when I first came to Germany in the Army and kept in touch through the years. I recognized his German-accented English on the other end immediately. Wilfried said his doctor had a vehicle to give us, but we should know, if we wanted it, that the motor was blown and it's a VW van. I pondered: *Should I take it, Lord?*

The question Wilfred posed brought both expectation and obligation to a new level of trust in God. Although we believed God would somehow provide us with a vehicle, we had not expected it to come with expenses.

Nevertheless, I got all the details. The thought that our castle auto shop kept six VW vans operational and in good repair gave me hope that this idea might work. I told him I would pray, get some more information and call back.

I wondered if owning the vehicle was biting off more than I could chew.

We had nothing in the bank, living strictly on incoming gifts from month to month. I prayed, *God, if You can provide a million dollars by faith for Don Stephens to buy a ship, you can provide $1,000 for us to buy a good motor for this vehicle.* I felt it was a statement as much as it was a request. My faith was the size of a mustard seed, defined in Matthew 17:20. Julie and I prayed together whether to accept Wilfried's offer.

After a few minutes … we decided *YES*!

John Babcock operated the auto maintenance and repair shop for all castle vehicles in the nearby town of Schwabmuenchen. He usually kept four to five VW motors on hand to rebuild. John said he had a 1600cc VW pancake Porsche engine he'd just rebuilt. I could purchase it on time in exchange for the blown motor and pay $1,000 for it as the extra funds came in. John would use my blown motor to train more mechanics. So, we rented a van, loaded up John's rebuilt VW motor and drove to Maintal (suburb of Frankfurt) to install it into our newly gifted van.

Having owned a VW bug and a VW van before, I had the mechanical skills to switch out the two motors in a couple of hours. It was a marvelous gift, and we celebrated God's provision for us. We paid off the VW in six months and drove it for the next two years, thanking God for His response to our prayers of faith.

21

A Communist Meets the Savior

OUR SECOND VISIT TO the Soviet Union grew from our desire to work with George Otis, Jr. and Issachar Strategic Missions in their effort to evangelize Russia in 1979. We would become part of an army of 5,000 Christians. God would lead each of us in our own prayer time on how, when, and where we would enter Russia, and, what we would do.

Julie and I prayed about joining this evangelistic effort, sensing that God wanted us to share our vision with our prayer partners and estimated our three-week trip to Russia would cost around $600. Knowing that Jesus said, *"All the angels in heaven rejoice over one soul who repents,"* Luke 15:10 (NIV), we deemed the time dedicated and the funds required minuscule compared to a lost soul finding Jesus for eternity.

God's economy is not our economy.

While praying for finances, we made preparation to go. Just a few days before departure, I found a box of Russian Bibles in the backroom of the castle library attic.

Recalling the book, *God's Smuggler,* and how Brother Andrew took thousands of copies of Bibles across Communist borders during the 1960s and 70s, I carried the box home, planning to take it with us. Tom Bragg, our castle publisher, was happy to get these Bibles into the hands of Russian Christians.

I really hadn't prayed much about taking the Russian Bibles with us. If I'm honest, I believe my heart filled with pride wanting to do what Brother Andrew did.

Julie wasn't in favor of bringing them, but I turned her a deaf ear. *Was God was trying to speak to me through my wife?*

Before we left, Jim and Ann Mills approached Julie and me, smiling and handed us an envelope full of Deutsch Marks. They gave us the equivalent of $450! It completed the total amount that we had prayed for.

According to George Otis' vision, over 5,000 Christians would make entries into the Soviet Union at different times over a three-month period, crossing over borders spread over thousands of miles. From Finland, down through the Soviet Pact nations of East Germany, Poland, Czechoslovakia, Hungary, the Balkans, Rumania, Bulgaria, Yugoslavia, Georgia, Armenia and Azerbaijan.

Our Christian coalition would be an invisible army to the border guards checking passports and visas since we went in one at a time through different checkpoints. We were confident God had a divine plan for each of us posing as tourists. Every person had their own map, destination, time of departure and arrival, and funding. George titled our invasion behind the Iron Curtain, '*Operation Friendship*.'

George Otis instructed these missionaries in groups of 10 - 50 all over Europe for over a year. Our group spent three days studying what to do, things not to do, necessary information we should know about Soviet law, culture, history, and methods of evangelism. He told us what we should do if detained by border patrol and how to contact the American Embassy in Moscow if needed.

The 1,300-mile trip to Odessa, Ukraine with our 18-month-old daughter Rachael would take us four to five days traveling over bumpy un-improved roads across Communist countries. We prayed for God's protection as we crossed the Leuşeni, Moldavian border (We'd decided that Leuşeni would be a good place to enter because we were there back in May 1975; it was familiar).

When we arrived, however, everything began going downhill. Nothing proved easy. Border guards separated us for hours of interrogation – "Why were we coming to Odessa?" They trashed through our suitcases inspecting every piece of clothing in front of the other tourists waiting in line for their turn. They accused us of working with the CIA, doing everything possible to intimidate us.

Tears flowed down Julie's face; Rachael bawled and needed her diaper changed ... by the time we were together again we felt naked and helpless. Then they made us stand outside our car while they took it apart piece by piece, removing the panels covering all four doors and finding nothing. A sinister looking man dressed wearing black attire and black gloves hustled out of a side building with a wooden case full of long wires with hooks. He dismantled the rear taillights and then inserted three and four-feet long wire hooks through the back taillight cavities. By this time, the sun was setting. It was still hot at 96 degrees temperature and sweat soaked through our days-old worn clothes.

Julie pitifully looked at me while swarms of mosquitoes feasted upon us.

"Ah-ha!" screamed a guard, holding up the Russian Bibles he'd found, *"Biblia, Biblia,"* scowling at me and gratified he'd found them carefully hidden in the inner small pockets. Other men in black coats now surrounded us.

I noted no other tourists were under this kind of scrutiny. *Had we been randomly picked for the search? Could they have known about our true mission to Russia?* Already detained at the border crossing for nearly eight hours now, I told the guard we wanted to leave and go back to Romania. The inspectors escorted us to the Customs Bureau office.

After two hours of more interrogation, the man in charge wanted me to sign a document in Russian. It didn't matter if I couldn't read it, they wanted us to confess we had tried to bring contraband into their country and that I had violated the laws of the Soviet Union. What I did was criminal! The guards treated us as if we were importing nuclear bombs. Amused European tourists stood in line observing the guards' fanatical behavior. They scorned the guards harassing us.

"What? The nation of Russia is scared to death of a few Bibles? We have millions of them in Europe and no one is afraid of them!"

I demanded our passports back. They refused so I said: "I'm calling the American Embassy!" They didn't like the sound of involving the U.S. government, so they gave us back our passports. On returning to our car, we found it left dismantled and it took an hour to restore all the pieces before we were able to drive away.

Weary to the bone, we retraced our path back to the Romanian border where we were welcome—such a different attitude they had toward us.

The Romanian guards told us they loved Americans and hated the Russians. They asked us if we watched the TV show *Miami Vice?* Julie and I cracked up over that question, our first laugh in the last 12 hours since we'd left Romania.

We checked in for the night at a five-star hotel for 30 dollars.

After signing the register and surrendering our passports, we learned that the water was in-operable and the elevators were 'temporarily' out of order. Handing us three metal buckets to fill for toilet use, the guy at reception told us to draw water from the Fountain of Lenin in the beautifully adorned floral courtyard, then carry the buckets through the lobby and up the four flights of stairs to our room.

As you might expect, we hand-bathed with cold water, splashing and laughing as we froze. Afterwards, we filled the toilet tanks with the rest of the water. Falling asleep, I thought: *Strange, I wonder why the Lenin water fountain is operating perfectly?*

Awoken at six a.m. by loud voices coming from four stories below on the street, I spied people lining up for two blocks, pushing and shoving to maintain their place in line. We could not imagine what the fuss was all about. Five minutes later, our answer came. A small panel truck pulled up for its daily distribution of bread. The handouts ran out, leaving about one third of the hungry people with nothing … it was a pitiful sight. Such is life under a Communist regime with its empty promises.

I realized I should have prayed a lot more before attempting to bring hidden Bibles into Russia, and asked Julie's forgiveness for not giving attention to her intuition. *God, forgive me and redeem this situation … can You bring any good out of what I've done?* It was hard for me to imagine how much trouble a few Bibles could cause.

We took our time returning home to Germany. As we passed through Budapest, Hungary, we decided I would ask a man working at a newspaper stand for directions to the farmers market. When walking away, a young lady came up to me, touched my arm and said, "Are you American? I heard you speaking English."

"Yes," I replied to her, shocked that she spoke such good English.

"Are you vacationing in our country with your family?"

"Yes, my wife and I just came into the city."

She smiled and continued, "Well, sir, I am Margo and my husband, Andrew, and I just came from the Balaton from vacation and we're on our way home. We have a few days before we return to work and we'd love to show you around our beautiful city and countryside. You can stay with us in our home. We really like Americans and would like to learn more about your country."

Normally, I would be on alert and leery of such an offer. George Otis, Jr. warned us to watch out for kidnappers and muggers. I went to Julie and told her about the young lady's invitation and pointed her out standing by the news stand.

Julie was skeptical at first, so we prayed about the offer. She felt it might be God guiding us to someone who was searching. *Maybe our journey was purposed for a time such as this?* We decided the risk was worth it, so we accepted the offer and invited Margo and Andrew into our van. They guided us through the streets of Budapest while describing the history of sites and buildings. Margo said, "In 1873, when two million inhabitants from three cities merged into one, Budapest became Hungary's capitol."

We learned that Margo had been trained as a tour guide for Hungary and Andrew was a computer programmer for IBM. Both were members of the Communist Party. She talked far more than her husband, sharing volumes of interesting history about their country. She reminded me of Judy Garland in *The Wizard of Oz*, only she had pitch black hair. Andrew was tall, long-haired, and highly intelligent, often twisting his mustache as he spoke.

We arrived at their home on the seventh floor of one of the old WWII gray concrete prefab apartment complexes. The ancient elevators opened two inches below the floor level but worked. The building's marble floors made a nice contrast to the ugly appearance of the dilapidated exterior.

Their compact, two-bedroom apartment was surprisingly charming, filled with many Western appliances they'd purchased on the black market. The couple were eager to build a friendship with us as travel outside of Hungary was forbidden to them.

But they treated us like family.

The American movies they'd seen had given them such a distorted view of average Americans; we were their first chance to find out what Americans were really like.

Julie and I were pleased with their honesty, transparency, and voracious curiosity about America. For three days we celebrated life together in the castles, palaces, bridges, churches, and enormous edifices built along the Danube River.

No visiting dignitary ever received such a royal treatment as they gave us.

After our Hungarian patriots extolled the virtues of Communism, they asked us what we believed about the future and the purpose of life. This was the opening we'd hoped for! Over breakfast, I began to share about our lives, our purpose, and our heart's desire to know God and share His love with others.

Julie told Margo of her journey as a young woman finding faith in God.

Margo had never read the Bible. I grabbed mine from the suitcase and for three hours poured over the scriptures with her; the prophecies about Jesus in the Old Testament and their fulfillment in the New Testament in the coming of Jesus.

Andrew sat apart from us on the couch while Margo hung on every word with an intensity that astonished me. She looked at her husband, huge tears formed around her eyes, and announced she wanted to ask Jesus to come into her heart and forgive her … and was he okay with that? When Andrew said he was not so convinced, but she could do whatever she wanted, he added, "I will love you no matter what you believe."

Margo bowed her head and said she went to a Catholic church once when she was small and told God, if He was real, to send someone to teach her how to know Him.

"It must have been God who sent you here this weekend. I somehow knew I should invite you to our home when I saw you at the news stand." Julie and I both teared up too. I led Margo in praying the same words I prayed when I invited Christ into my life at 18 and God graciously forgave her and entered her heart.

We gave Margo scripture studies and a Bible to begin learning God's Word and encouraged her to find an underground church that taught the Bible, in order to grow in her faith. God made her a new creation that day. "*Yet to all who received Him, who believed on his Name, he gave the right to become the children of God." John 1:12 (NIV)* Perhaps our rejection at the Soviet border was God's plan all along. We will only know when we get to heaven.

22

The Budapest Treasure Hunt

LIVING IN A 17th CENTURY castle in southern Germany has its perks. The magnificent view of the Bavarian Alps through the sixth-story attic window that morning was remarkable.

The foothills of the Alps were covered with fresh fallen pristine snow. A patchwork of family farm dwellings dotted the landscape; their roofs frosted in white.

I sighed at the beauty of it all.

It had been a year since our trip to the Russian border. Julie was six months pregnant with our second child and we needed to increase our income to pay our rent. We'd recently returned from the States where we'd made our bi-annual fundraising visit. I panned back through the memories of our time in Eaton, Ohio. Julie's father, Al, insistied I meet their friends, Robert and Ruth Miller, who owned the world's largest and rarest private Hummel collection. So, I went just to make him happy.

When Al and I visited Robert, he gave me a history lesson regarding the highly desired German-crafted ceramic figurines. "The rarest ones were marketed to the Eastern Bloc nations (former Communist states of Eastern and Central Europe) before World War II as test-market samples of cultural traditional festive dress in Bulgarian, Romanian, Hungarian, Yugoslavian and Czech. When World War II started they never made it to mass production because all borders closed."

From his collection of thousands of Hummels, Robert showed me five pre-WWII Hummels worth over $250,000. My head swooned.

What if I visited that flea market in Budapest just to take a look around?

If Robert had purchased five Hummels found there a couple of years ago, maybe a few more were still remaining at the same flea market for sale now.

Then Robert dropped the clincher. "And Dixey, if you happen to find, '*The Good Shepherd*', #42 II, I will send you a check for $6,000!"

My father-in-law looked at me with a knowing glint in his eyes. He knew I had swallowed the bait.

Why should I not be the one to make a 'great discovery'?

I'm always up for an adventure. *Is this of God? Is this the proper use of our time and money? How could God not want me to do this?*

Negative voices bombarded my thoughts, too. I countered those thoughts with positive thinking. *If I found The Good Shepherd Hummel, Julie and I would use the money for God's work and not for personal consumption.*

The fact that my dad was willing to obtain a loan for me, and my father-in-law offering his support, further reinforced the idea of proceeding with my effort. I had faith in God to help me. "*Now faith is the substance of things hoped for, the evidence of things not seen.*" Hebrews 11:1(KJV). I started planning for my hopeful future discovery.

When we returned to Germany, I organized my trip. We'd exchanged our VW van for an upgrade to a more-comfy lime-green French Citroen station wagon a month before. I readied for the 16-hour round trip to Budapest, praying the newer car had no unknown problems and would not break down.

As I walked toward the car, Julie said, "Dixey, I believe that you are to go to that marketplace … I have a peace in my heart."

I kissed Julie goodbye and began the 325-mile drive on the autobahn through Munich and Salzburg. The beautiful Austrian alpine scenery ended at a long line of cars and trucks stopped at the Austrian-Hungarian border control crossing. Having traveled these roads before, I knew what to expect. A two to three hour wait at the Customs Bureau, a car search inspection, then the issue of my tourist visa.

In 1980 the antiquated governmental systems of paperwork lines, multiple offices and personnel stamping all kinds of papers signified the ineptitude and bureaucratic chaos of the Communist system.

Finally, after hours of waiting, I passed over the border. On arrival, I did not know where to find the Budapest flea market, so I went to the Information Bureau at the main train station. They always know everything. A kind lady speaking broken German drew me a map of the area. I saw that the flea market was only six miles away.

Some sections of old Budapest are unbelievably beautiful but driving through the outskirts of the city revealed rows of poorly constructed prefab, soot polluted, tall apartment complexes lining the neighborhoods.

I stopped at the complex of Margo and Andrew where we had stayed the previous year. Sadly, they had moved, leaving no forwarding address with their neighbors. The buildings were similarly painted in drab colors and appeared unsafe for occupancy. Not far from the residential area, smokestacks on industrial complex buildings barreled out pillars of toxic smoke, diluting the city's beauty even more.

I arrived at the flea market about 10 p.m., parked the car off the road and slept inside. After tossing and turning throughout the night, morning came with the rising sun blinding my eyes. I ventured out and saw sidewalk food vendors selling steamed, young-picked field corn for breakfast. I could not pass by the aroma of the fresh Hungarian walnut and pistachio *baklava torts* and *Kurtoskalacs* (chimney cakes) Hungary is famous for.

Hundreds of wood shanties along the aisles were packed with every imaginable article: chandeliers, 100-year-old porcelain headed dolls, kilned-baked painted clay vases with every possible sculptural design, clothes, scarves, jewelry, windows, door hinges, hardware, furniture, huge-framed mirrors, paintings and more.

Antiques were the most popular items. The smaller shops were sectioned off by dirt walking paths, giving the market a sense of order. My goal was to find an extremely rare Hummel with the crown stamp on its base.

I prayed, "*Lord, I ask that You direct my steps today. Amen!*"

After visiting some 30 shops over the next three hours, I wondered if I should have concocted this whole scheme. If I don't find it, I am going to owe the spent money from dad for a good while. *Why do I dream up these crazy ideas?* I continued my search through another dozen shops as discouragement began to set in. *How does one go about finding a needle in a haystack?*

I finally entered a shop that featured many kinds of figurines. I saw a couple of Hummels which brightened my spirit, but none of them were of WWII vintage – they were newer – and they didn't have the Crown Bee stamp.

Perusing every counter and aisle, I glimpsed a small door partially open, almost hidden from view, behind a stack of boxes. I did not want to appear too eager as vendors were known to raise their prices on the spot if they thought your heart was set on something, so I milled around a bit longer.

"Is it alright for me to go through this door into the smaller room?"

He nodded his approval and switched on the light. As soon as I stepped inside, I nearly went into shock. To my left, on the tallest shelf, stood a row of neatly arranged Hummels, eight of them. I could scarcely believe my eyes … the tallest one in the middle was *The Good Shepherd*!

The price was $150 for one so I asked the owner, "Will you take $800 for all eight of them?" His frown turned into a smile. That is two months income in Hungarian forint currency. Before paying, I checked for the signature. *M. I. Hummel* incised on the back of the base of *The Good Shepherd,* including the incised crown mark on the bottom. I could hardly restrain from shouting. It was in perfect condition—no scratches, hairline cracks, porcelain fractures, no crazing or chips.

Number 42 II was the exact figurine Robert Miller tasked me to find in Budapest … and I did! The other Hummels also had the crown marks (Made Circa, 1935) and were signed also.

As I record that historic event now, the same feelings of awe return when I first held *The Good Shepherd* in my hands. Not knowing it would be there, I only surmise that God must have directed me. I perused the rest of the flea market and found nothing else.

I packed my valuable find that day, safely wrapped in the back of the car, and made my way back home. On return, my smile and bags betrayed my find! Julie let out a whoop! I immediately phoned Mr. Miller.

Three months had passed since we'd last spoken face-to-face. I almost shouted the words, "Bob, I've found *The Good Shepherd*! I've found *The Good Shepherd*!" Not recognizing my voice, he hung up!

Perplexed, I dialed his number again. "Robert, this is Dixey Behnken, the missionary in Germany. I've found your Hummel, the one you wanted – *The Good Shepherd,* you know, 42 II!"

"Oh, it's you, Dixey. It's two a.m. here in Ohio. I thought you were some skid-row derelict calling a wrong number. Someone telling me he'd gotten saved, that's why I hung up."

In the next few minutes, I shared with him how I found the valuable Hummel figurine alongside seven others. Since every Hummel had the WWII vintage crown stamps incised on them, Robert agreed to send me a check for $8,500 for all eight Hummels. God had come through! *The Good Shepherd* had wanted me to find '*The Good Shepherd* Hummel!' – with God's blessing!

I felt like I'd won the lottery! But why had God provided me more money than I had ever seen or held before?

23

The Wind Blows Wherever It Wishes

YOU WILL RECALL WHEN I graduated Miami University three years earlier, we considered going straight to seminary, but I had tired of books. Even back then, the idea of becoming an Army Chaplain had crossed my mind several times, but the thought of the four-year task of seminary studies overwhelmed me.

Now at 30, I sensed the calling getting stronger. I knew to become an Army Chaplain that a Master of Divinity degree was required. I was not the only one who felt I should go to seminary.

Rev. Donald Kirkby, a retired Presbyterian minister on staff at the castle accompanied me on a retreat where I spoke in Regensberg, Germany. Don's counsel and wisdom was esteemed throughout YWAM. Two of his adult children, Allen and Annette, also served in YWAM missions in Europe. On our return home, before starting the car, Don turned, looked at me seriously and smiled, "Dixey, God has His hand on you. Have you ever sensed a desire to go to seminary?" When Don said that, something clicked. We discussed the idea all the way back to the castle.

When I shared about this old direction renewing its fire with Julie, and what Don said to me, she agreed. I had often considered studying under Dr. Robert Coleman, Asbury Seminary's Professor of Discipleship and Evangelism. He preached powerfully in chapel back when I attended Asbury College in 1970.

"I'm feeling the same thing. It's time for you to hit the books again, I think it's a matter we really need to pray about."

* * *

A month later, Julie announced, "It's time to take me to the hospital, contractions are six minutes apart." Less than two hours later, she delivered a healthy boy, Lukas Frederick. I loved the book of Luke in the Bible and named him after the German spelling. His middle name came from my dad and granddad's middle name. *Would God make him a missionary like us?*

* * *

A year later while praying with our leaders, it felt right to return home for more studies. It turns out that God's provision from the Hummels dovetailed with a number of matters coming in our future. It would pay back dad's loan, cover all of our expenses during our remaining year in the mission field, provide our flight tickets home, purchase of a vehicle and cover my first three semesters' tuition attending Asbury Theological Seminary in Wilmore, Kentucky.

My dad collected us from the Dayton Airport. In the car, we began catching up on recent news as my mom held Lukas in the back seat beaming with joy! The exhausting long travel from the castle took its toll, and both Julie and Rachael fell asleep. While driving, dad handed me a name and address and asked:

"Do you remember this fellow?"

"Sure, I do, Hector Perez Chavez, my first convert from street preaching in Mexico City ten years ago!"

"Well, while you were in Germany, God has been doing great things through him in Oaxaca. You must have really impacted his life."

"How on earth did you get his current address dad? I lost touch with him about five years ago. My letters came back to me."

"My lifelong friend, Bob Shank came by the store last week and told me he bumped into him in Oaxaca, where the Shanks vacation every year. They visited a new church there and Hector greeted them at the door. Recognizing they were Americans, he inquired if they knew Dixey Behnken from Brookville, Ohio in America? Well, you can imagine their response. Hector passed word through them to greet you and give you this card!" It read:

"Dixey, thank you for coming to Mexico City ten years ago and leading me to Jesus Christ. If you ever return to Mexico City, come down to Oaxaca to visit with us. I started a church that has grown to over 500 believers who love and serve Jesus. I'm sure they'd like to thank you too!"

We shook our heads in amazement. My preaching on the street and follow-up letters had created a faithful disciple. The Apostle Paul's greatest joy were those whom he led to Christ. My heart glowed upon hearing the news. I have no doubt that Hector and I shall meet again in heaven, if not before.

24

Seminary's Surprises

I DID NOT ONLY EARN a Master's Degree in seminary, Julie also added two more wonderful children; Hope Rayanne and Brandon David to our family. To help with our additional expenses, I worked at Pizza Hut washing pots and pans, cleaning chimneys on weekends, and driving a school bus three times a day.

I also made application to get a commission with the Kentucky Army National Guard for the position of Chaplain Candidate (2LT), Staff Specialist.

We were quite disappointed when a letter came back two months later stating *Please apply again next year, all allocations are filled.* The following year I applied again. This time a letter came stating, *Report to the Kentucky National Guard State Office in Louisville for commissioning to Second Lieutenant on August 3, 1983.*

My apprenticeship under Chaplain (Major) Gene Strange with the 138th Field Artillery Brigade in Lexington, set the forces in motion steering me toward becoming an active-duty Army Chaplain. His exemplary leadership and watching how he built relationships with Soldiers became my model for the future.

In the meantime, Dr. Robert Coleman's classes over the three and a half years at Asbury greatly intensified my personal evangelism drive. Additionally, the Senior class bestowed the honor of selecting me to present a sermon in chapel to the entire seminary for our Senior graduation week.

After preaching, Dr. John M. Vayhinger, the Seminary Psychologist, approached me and said, "Dixey, you need to write a book and share your stories with the world." His words have germinated for 37 years … -this book is finally the result of the seed he planted.

To top it off, at graduation in May 1984, the seminary announced my induction into the Theta Phi International Theological Honor Society.

25

Staring Death in the Face

IN JUNE 1984, AFTER graduating Asbury Seminary in Wilmore, Kentucky, we moved back near Brookville, Ohio, into my grandmother Kuck's home on Diamond Mill Road. Grandma had passed away at the age of 95 a few months before my graduation, leaving the house empty. We had started the application process for my commission into the U. S. Army Chaplaincy but had no idea how long it would take for my application to get approved.

I recall the 33 forms I had to fill out for the massive process. One balmy afternoon the six of us loaded into the car and headed east toward Trotwood on Little Richmond Road for a visit with our cousins. Our four children had snuggled quietly into their seats for the ride. The stretch of county road we travelled was marked with double yellow no-passing lanes that spooled across the numerous hills and valleys that are typical in the region. Often, you cannot see oncoming traffic hidden by the hills. Julie and I were making small talk, when suddenly, I faced a life-or-death decision. Two vehicles came racing toward us in a dead heat.

The car in my lane came straight for us side-by-side with the car he was trying to pass cresting the top of the hill. With only seconds until the inevitable impact, I stared death in the face once again, just as I had on my motorcycle 17 years before. This time it wasn't just my life on the line; what would happen to my entire family?

Slamming on my brakes was not an option; that would guarantee a collision with the oncoming car. Either I would stay in the right lane where I'm supposed to be and pray that the other car in my lane moved further right into a wide shallow ditch to bypass me, or I take the ditch, and let the oncoming car continue passing me. With no time to signal any kind of intention, my split-second action would either doom us to a head-on collision or allow us to escape unharmed.

Julie froze in her seat, bracing for impact, and praying.

Ditch or stay? Ditch or stay? I decided to stay and prayed the other car would take the ditch path ... which he did, suddenly swerving over into the ditch just seconds before our cars collided head-on. Once again, I felt the vacuuming *swoosh* passing between the two cars narrowly missing me! In my rearview mirror, the speeding car fishtailed out of the ditch and back onto the road, spewing dirt, dust, and debris.

Praise God! Coming away unscathed, except for our pounding hearts, frayed nerves, and the realization we could all have lost our lives.

I pulled the car over to the side of the road and shut off the motor. We prayed a prayer of thanksgiving. *God, You must have plans for our family that is far beyond anything I can imagine. Thank You for saving our lives. Please keep Your protective hand upon us and help us all to follow Your ways. In Jesus' name, Amen.*

We spent a few minutes talking about what had just happened, recovering from our fear and allowing our racing emotions to subside. Julie and I were surging with adrenalin, our bodies still shaking. Life is so random, and it can disappear quickly when one is not even contemplating a disaster. Death can occur so spontaneously.

Did God protect us, or did I just get lucky on a 50-50 chance? How did everything work out so perfectly?

26

The Face of an Angel

WHILE IN THE 307th Engineer Battalion, 82nd Airborne Division at Ft. Bragg, North Carolina, my ecclesiastical endorser, Chaplain Jim Ammerman, (Colonel-Retired) phoned me from Dallas. He asked if I would represent our denomination, *Chaplaincy of Full Gospel Churches (CFGC),* and speak at the Maranatha Church Convention in Florence, South Carolina. Since God had called me to become an Army Chaplain, Jim wanted me to share with them about CFGC chaplaincy work concerning the opportunity to align their churches under CFGC representation so they could provide their ministers to the Pentagon as future chaplains.

On October 5th, 1986, after sharing my message and stepping down from the stage, I was approached by a jubilant young lady around 20 years of age who was ecstatic over my message. Her joyful countenance and enthusiasm for the Lord was infectious. I made a mental note of her name, Terri Grey, as she rapidly spoke about her love for Jesus, her desire to become a missionary and in six months her plans of joining a mission team. Terri went on to say her boyfriend had also attended Airborne School in the Air Force.

Aha! That's it! I thought. *That's what has put a glow on her face! She's in love!* There was no other explanation for the *remarkable angelic glow* on her face.

I would never forget meeting her.

After speaking with several others at the service, another woman, about 70 years old, said: "Chaplain Behnken, I cannot believe what I just witnessed. I am a long-time member of the church and remembered Terri first attending here when she was 14 years old. I don't know what it was that you said to her tonight, but I've never seen anything like it before." I wondered what she meant.

She said, "Do you know who I mean, Terri Grey?"

"Yes, I do. I just spoke to her for 15 minutes." *The visual of the glow on Terri's face was still strongly in my memory.*

"After you talked with Terri, she shared with me how excited she was about your message and service to the Lord in the military. You must have said something very special that touched her in an unusual way. *Her face is glowing like an angel's face tonight.*"

I thought to myself, *this is really unusual.* I was not the only one who noted the glow on Terri's face. There was something mysterious and divine about it.

I doubt that Terri realized how she glowed when sharing her love for God's work.

The following morning, I was seated in the kitchen of an elegant home. My hosts were elders in the congregation of about 600 members. The church had a Bible School and educational wing attached to it. The phone rang and my host, Diane, picked up the receiver. I overheard her comment back to the caller:

"Oh, no, no, no, not Terri Grey!" I listened more intently to catch more details of what happened to Terri. Diane finished the call and looked at me in tears.

"Terri Grey has gone to be with the Lord."

What? No! I couldn't believe it – it's not possible! I'd only known her for a few minutes, tears fell from my eyes while trying to absorb the terrible news.

"Dixey, do you know what that caller just told me? She had spoken with Terri last night and she mentioned that "*Terri's face was glowing like an angel.*""

The person who phoned Diane was the *third* person who saw *Terri's glowing face.*

Last night Terri had exhibited God's presence in a way that is rare. I recalled how in the Bible there was *a glow on Moses' face* after he came down from the mountain carrying the Ten Commandments after speaking to God.

Some people have the mindset that religious people are somewhat given over to exaggeration, that Christians are naïve and see life through rosy colored glasses. They think we are easily swayed or conditioned to believe in supernatural events.

Unfortunately, at times, that may be true.

But after hearing this story, you may feel differently. "Terri had the heart of a servant," Diane said. "My friend just told me that after Terri helped the night's cleanup crew and breakfast prep crews in the large picnic tent after the meeting last night, she left the church to go home around midnight."

I tensed, "What happened?"

"Terri's car was found by a passing motorist off the road about an hour later. She fell asleep at the wheel, crashed into a ditch, was thrown out and the car rolled over on top of her."

As you might imagine, when we got to the church, the mood at the annual convention was sorrowful as word spread about Terri's accident. The sudden loss of a wonderful Christian young person dedicated to becoming a missionary shocked everyone. While Christians have hope for a better life and the assurance that life does not end at the grave, I took great comfort in the Apostle Paul's words in I Thessalonians, 4:13 (NIV), "*We do not want you to be uninformed about those who sleep in death, so that you do not grieve like the rest of mankind, who have no hope."*

The pastor opened the evening service with: "Tonight, we are going to honor Sister Terri with a celebration of praise for her life." The worship team led with songs and 10 ladies danced in procession down the church aisles, singing and waving their colorful flags. As they surrounded the altar, they symbolically welcomed Terri into her heavenly home. Afterwards the pastor shared his insights.

He'd received the 2:45 a.m. phone call notifying him of Terri's accident. Knowing where she lived, he'd traced the path to get to the scene.

Approaching the car, the wrecker operator greeted him while removing the car off of her body. This was a task the operator had done more times than he cared to remember. He tried to prepare the pastor for the bloody scene he was about to see when the car was lifted. But as the car rolled off Terri's body, both the pastor and wrecker operator were amazed at what they saw—absolutely no blood was upon Terri's body! She had no gashes, bruises, nor physical mangling from the weight of the car.

"Look!" the operator pointed at Terri's body. "Look at her face, pastor! *She has the glow of an angel on her face!*" The pastor had never seen anything like it.

The paramedics took Terri's body from the wreckage, a coroner pronounced her dead, and her body was moved to the morgue.

"Church, everyone at the site of the accident was amazed by what we witnessed." The pastor then pointed to the back of the church. "In fact, the operator of the wrecker service and the paramedics who attended to Terri, are here tonight and sitting in the back row. They wanted to visit the church where she attended, honor her life, and hear the message I have prepared, to send Terri on to her new heavenly mission."

Another man stood at the back of the church. He was an older fellow, dressed in a baggy orange suit and surrounded by two policemen. At a closer look you'd see the chains around his wrists, waist and ankles bound together. This man had come from prison to attend the service.

The pastor told how at age 14, Terri was removed from her home and placed under foster care, because on numerous occasions her father had sexually molested her. He'd been convicted and was serving a 20-year sentence. Terri recorded in her personal journal that she started praying for her father to come to Jesus and repent of his sins. One of Terri's prayers from her journal, given to him by Terri's foster parents, reads: "*I forgive you, father. Over and over, I've forgiven you for the last seven years.*"

Terri's foster parents had loved her dearly and shared with the audience how Terri sang like a songbird. They'd often heard her at bedtime, crying out loud, prayers for her father.

At the close of the service, the pastor clearly explained how Christ forgives sin, offers a new life, a new family, and a new future to all who repent.

"Terri had fulfilled Christ's commission by committing her life to missionary work. She is no longer with us and won't be going to the mission field. But I believe God will choose someone else to go in her place. If God is placing His call upon your life, please come forward so we can dedicate you to the Lord."

One by one, students who had studied alongside Terri stood up from all over the church and made their way to the front. They received *the call.* Ten young men and women committed to become missionaries that night to 'Go into all the world' and share the love of Christ.

The pastor concluded, "I believe it would honor the Lord to invite anyone here to come forward tonight who senses that God is calling you to follow Christ." The wrecker operator, who had never been in a church service before, walked down the aisle. Following him was the stranger – Terri's father – the man in the orange prison uniform accompanied by the two police officers. He walked forward and kneeled to pray to receive the forgiveness of Jesus. His life was changed because he felt forgiveness and acceptance from the love of God.

Some of Terri's friends knelt beside her father and prayed. Terri's earnest prayer *that her father would find Jesus* was answered in her death.

This event occurred early in my chaplain career. Confronted by such a devastating, horrendous experience, one that does not meet the 'common sense' test, is a tough pill to swallow – spiritually and theologically. The best answers do not begin to satisfy our deepest unanswered questions … and never will. A biblical prophet speaks to our ineptitude in explaining the mysteries of this life. From Isaiah 55:8-9 (NASB) we read: *"For My thoughts are not your thoughts. Nor are your ways My ways," declares the Lord. "For as the heavens are higher than the earth, so are My ways higher than your ways. And My thoughts than your thoughts."*

For some reason, the answers are not always given to us by our Lord. In closing this chapter, I encourage you to look up the words in the hymn that has always given me comfort which I discovered in seminary, "How Firm A Foundation." They have never failed to lift my heart, my sorrow or my confusion.

27

Hohenfels Combat Maneuver Training Center

AFTER TWO YEARS JUMPING out of airplanes and training with my Soldiers at Ft. Bragg, orders to 2-64 Armor Battalion came for us to move overseas to Schweinfurt, Germany. I was already familiar with the life of a tanker in Germany, having done it for over three years in 1971-1974.

Our move to Schweinfurt was exciting and thankfully uneventful having Julie and four kids in tow. My newly assigned tank battalion often trained at Hohenfels, Germany, where weather conditions during rainy and winter seasons were not ideal.

The sites were either plagued with dust and mud or ice and snow. Each training rotation lasted for three to five weeks at a time. My unit executed tank battle engagements and maneuver exercises. Watching dozens of 67-ton Abrams descend upon their prey at 40 miles an hour is a sight to behold.

Hohenfels Combat Maneuver Training Center (CMTC) has been the joint multinational center for training NATO troops and Armies worldwide. At this location, the U.S. military and other armed forces use the Multiple Integrated Laser Engagement System, or 'MILES', for training purposes. This system uses lasers and blank cartridges to simulate actual combat in battle.

I sometimes rode in the Company Commander's tank, making it a point to pray with the crew before battle exercises began. On other occasions, I rode inside sitting in the gunner and loader's seats, popping my head out of the Tank Commander's hatch to keep abreast of our situation. On other occasions, I left the motor pool and drove my thin-skinned Humvee to visit troops bivouacked out in the fields. Operating tanks demanded constant attention to safety; situations could easily turn dangerous in training maneuvers.

Our simulated tank wars were spread out over 52 square miles. Rommel's tanks trained on this same terrain for WWII in 1938. As part of an army team engaging the OPFOR (OPposition FORces), I was thrilled as we rolled through fields, hills, and valleys in an M1 Abrams tank flanked by another 12 tanks abreast. Whenever the enemy fired lasers at us, we fired back.

The 2-64 Armor Battalion was my fourth unit assignment since my chaplaincy began in 1985. I soon became an integral part of the command military team and a vital force multiplier for morale among the Soldiers. My job was to counsel, spiritually uplift the troops, advise the Commander and provide religious services.

I often brought refreshments, canisters of coffee or soup, to the 400 Soldiers in an effort to establish good rapport with them. I found them scattered throughout the forests and battlefield in smaller groups. Their gracious smiles welcomed me.

Once, when the temperature had dropped below zero, we stumbled upon a Mortar Track, an M113, that had lost power for over 36 hours. It was one of ours. With tank batteries dead, the crew could not communicate with their Commander to establish a location. Rescue was impossible. All they needed was a tank recovery vehicle, a Hercules M88, to come and get them.

I rattled my canteen cup against the hatchback door of their M113 while holding a jug of hot coffee in the other hand. Soon, four freezing Soldiers appeared. With gracious smiles, amidst clouds of steamy breath, they roared:

"It's the Chaplain! You won't believe this, but we actually prayed an hour ago that somebody would come our way and rescue us. We were freezing, and just look—it's you!" Sometimes it's the small things that you do for others that they remember the most. They were joyful as I served them hot coffee and handed over a radio microphone to call in their grid coordinates. My visit spared them from hours in the freezing temperatures … or perhaps worse.

After eight months of serving in my unit, I discovered another reason for the Soldier's smiles on my arrival. The previous chaplain did not have a vehicle. A politically savvy Senior Maintenance NCO outmaneuvered him and commandeered his vehicle. This leaves the chaplain with no option except to hitch rides everywhere with tanks. I was advised to fight for my own vehicle since I had MTOE authorization. (I won't bore you with definitions of MTOE, TDA and TOE.) Fortunately, I convinced my Commander of the importance of a chaplain having the vehicle purposed for the chaplain's job.

"Go get it, chaplain!" he told me. He informed the Executive Officer (XO) who executed the transfer and now the vehicle came under my control.

I eagerly signed for my entitled Humvee. Somehow, the troops in the Battalion knew I was coming before I got there. They were always laughing when I arrived.

I couldn't figure out why. A few days later, I discovered a Soldier had painted a large playboy bunny silhouette on top of my roof in the camouflage colors of brown, black, tan, and green. Later, when someone pointed out the emblem, I asked my chaplain assistant to repaint a regular camouflage pattern over it. That was one problem solved. Sometimes a chaplain must fight for his or her miracles.

28

Soldier's Don't Fly

ON A COLD NOVEMBER evening, inside a Post Chapel, a supernatural experience beyond my wildest dreams took me by surprise. Since graduating seminary, I had read 15-20 books about demons and angels. There have been a lot of mysteries and strange occurrences recorded in different foreign lands and religions over the centuries.

My own experience as a missionary in Germany for four years alerted me to people plagued by occultic influences. However, nothing I'd read or seen up close prepared me for what I would encounter before this night ended. From reading how Jesus, Peter and the disciples and other followers of 'the Way' faced evil entities as described in the gospels and Book of Acts, I knew the basic principles of how evil manifested itself in humanity and how to deal with it.

As seminary students, we had studied *hamartiology* (doctrine of sin), *demonology*, *angelology,* and *soteriology* (doctrine of salvation). This particular evening would unfold in such a climax that both angelic and demonic power realms would stake their claim. When two opposing forces in the supernatural realm collide, it is usually over a human life, a family, and sometimes over a city or a nation.

Somehow, humans are central in a cosmic conflict where one force is *for us*, and the opposite force *against us*. (An astute *Star Wars* theologian (sic) would certainly agree.) These life forces are with us from the day we are born until the day we die. None of us escape living in the middle of this cosmic conflict.

After concluding my evening Bible study on the authority of the believer, I had asked if anyone was interested in receiving personal ministry with the *laying on of hands*. In Christian churches, this practice is both symbolic and a formal method of invoking the Holy Spirit to work in a person's life. It primarily occurs during baptisms, church confirmations, healing services, dispensing of blessings, the ordination of priests, ministers, elders, deacons, and other church officers, along with a variety of other historic church sacraments and holy ceremonies.

There were 12 – 14 Soldiers in attendance that evening from some five tank battalions. They came in response to the fliers I'd posted out in the field training sites. They secured their weapons in a set location under guard since no weapons were allowed in chapels.

Dressed in mud laden BDUs (Battle Dress Uniforms), their hearts were amazingly spiritually open to a new touch from God. I prepared in the Spirit for that evening by fasting and praying for these troops.

God touched so many men's lives in our unit throughout the past year. I had seen many Soldiers experience a personal faith in Jesus Christ during our services. Healings and miracles had occurred under my watch, so my confidence level in God manifesting His presence this night was quite high.

The Post Chaplain, Chaplain Steve invited me to speak and lead the service. When serving as a guest chaplain on the base, it is important to agree on how the service will be conducted. After teaching a one-hour Bible study, I directed the attendees to kneel in a circle. We would seek God with lifted hands.

Chaplain Steve stood beside me as we made our way around the circle of Soldiers asking each one what they would like the Lord to do for them.

Some responded with, "Pray for me to be a stronger witness for Jesus among the Soldiers. There is a lot of temptation out there." Others said, "I would like to be prayed for to receive the "baptism of the Holy Spirit." Some wanted us to give them a word of personal prophecy by the gift of knowledge as affirmation from the Lord.

After praying for several men, I approached one young man and laid my hands on his head to pray for him. He looked up at me and said he wanted to receive Jesus. But, when he tried to speak the name of Jesus, he would choke. He could not say the name of Jesus. I had seen this before on several occasions. He also asked for us to pray for the infilling of the Holy Spirit. As I began praying for him, a weird expression crossed his face. He strangely said, "I cannot say that name of Je-___, of Jes-__, of Jesu-_." I asked him to repeat with me a prayer to invite Jesus into his life and to forgive his sins. As he tried to call out to Jesus for help, his eyes suddenly enlarged and filled with fear, rage, and terror. He screamed at the top of his lungs, as if in great pain. Everyone looked in shock at his aggressive behavior.

Before I could say or do anything else, he launched up at me from his kneeling position trying to grab my neck to choke me. In one moment, I was standing an arm's length from him with my hands resting on his head. In a flash, his hands and whole body were only inches from my neck. Stunned and feeling the need to defend myself, I could not move quickly enough to deflect his aggression. I just stood there petrified, waiting to receive the painful attack, but something else happened. It was as if an invisible force field came between me and my attacker. The other Soldiers recognized something bizarre was happening.

In a split second, the attacking Soldier shot backwards, high above everyone's head, right across the room as if he'd been shot out of a cannon! He struck the wall about 12 feet away at eye level and slumped to the floor.

One Soldier yelled, "What was that?"

Another exclaimed, "Did you see what I saw?"

We rushed over to see if he was hurt. Surprisingly, he was smiling. With eyes shut, he whispered, "Thank you, Jesus. Jesus, you are so wonderful ... hallelujah."

He no longer had a problem saying the name of 'Jesus'. When he opened his eyes, he was totally unaware of anything that had taken place.

He said, "I just wanted to get free from the spirits that my family worshipped and come to know Jesus. Then he noticed his surroundings and asked, "What am I doing slumped down over here by the wall?"

He explained that his mother was from Indonesia and worshipped ancestral spirits. As a sorceress, she possessed great powers in the occult world. He'd been terrified of his mother his entire life. I concluded the evil spirits from Indonesia that dominated his family for generations wanted to keep this Soldier enslaved as their property (their home).

In the Bible, demons refer to the body they inhabit as their 'home'. The spirits Jesus confronted in the Gerasene demoniac (Luke 8:26-38, Mark 5:12), repeatedly resisted leaving the body of a tormented man. They pleaded with Jesus not to cast them out of the man's body. "Where will we go?" they worried.

It has been my experience on occasion that some people afflicted with evil spirits cannot speak the name of Jesus. But after the Soldier's demons were expelled, he easily spoke the name of 'Jesus' praising and worshipping Him with great joy. This incident was unbelievable. Our minds tried to take in what we'd seen.

It was astonishing. The Bible speaks of guardian angels (Daniel 6:22, Psalm 34:7, Matthew 18:10).

Was it my guardian angel that acted to protect me?

This was a first and only time in my life where I visibly observed such an occurrence. This had not been part of my plan for *that* prayer meeting.

Soldiers don't fly. All I can attest to is that some invisible force protected me from that Soldier. I call this a miracle.

29

Other Strange Manifestations

AT ONE ARMY POST, after conducting three field services and speaking to Soldiers on applying God's power in breaking spiritual bondages, I woke up on a Monday morning, praying about my appointment with the Post Chaplain. I was into my second week of partial fasting and puzzled why Chaplain Jay had asked to see me.

Since taking over as chaplain in a newly assigned location, Chaplain Jay felt a strange evil presence everywhere he went, even in his home. He wanted me to pray for him. He had heard about 'the flying Soldier' story from Chaplain Steve.

He told me that the Post Commander, Colonel Schreiver, had ordered the Officers' Club Manager to hire strippers from a nearby German town to entertain officers on Saturday evenings. The revenue from the strippers lifted the Officers' Club debts out of the *red* and boosted his Soldier's morale. Chaplain Jay confronted Colonel Schreiver personally about unauthorized use of government funding for the strippers but was ignored. He continued his prayers against this misuse and abuse. Schreiver's wife wasn't happy about it and the other wives in the chapel supported her. He casually overrode their protests.

The strippers had performed on this post for the past six months. When Chaplain Jay objected to this degrading and illegal activity at the weekly Commander's staff meeting, he was overruled and chided by the other officers on the staff who attended the Officer's Club every weekend. Chaplain Jay invited me to preach the following Sunday. I wondered what part God wanted me to take in this matter.

As I left Chaplain Jay's office that day, I wondered what, if anything, I should do. This wasn't my post. We woke up the next morning to horrible news. A Company Commander's tank on a training maneuver here had flipped over, instantly pinning and killing three of the four tank crew. They'd tried to escape out the hatches, scrambling to get free of the tank rollover. Captain Smith, the Company Commander, was one of the dead.

His gunner and his driver were also killed. Only the loader survived the rollover. Even the best trained Soldiers often resort to a gut reaction and try to escape out the hatch during a tank rollover.

It was so dark the night before that the crew did not detect, even with their night vision goggles, the previously dug out 'hiding position' another tank had vacated. The tank had approached the dugout blindly, moving slowly, but unable to stop soon enough. With one track on land and the other suspended spinning in the air, it teetered, then flipped upside down into the 10-foot-deep garage-sized gorge.

The news grew even worse as I learned more about Captain Smith. He had a newborn child only weeks old and his family was scheduled to transition back to the States in just three weeks. Now, his wife and her newborn daughter would have to return home alone, with no husband, no father. Since the deaths occurred in a sister unit and not my unit, their chaplain performed the funeral.

I sought the Lord for an answer as to why He had allowed such a great loss of men and equipment. A scripture came to my mind. When I looked it up, I sensed that God held the leader of the training post responsible.

An accident of this kind is the one thing every unit Commander dreads. Nothing is so demoralizing as when a Commander loses Soldiers under his command. After proper notifications to families; memorial and funeral services follow. Then, the Army Investigation team becomes involved. It's their job to determine what happened, how it could have been avoided, and who is responsible.

30

Face Off with the Post Commander

COMMANDERS ARE SOMETIMES *relieved for cause.* They are held responsible for their troops and accountable to the highest standards of conduct. A Commander may be relieved of duty due to "loss of confidence in ability to command."

Other reasons include allegations of drunk driving, inappropriate personal relationships, mistreatment of Soldiers, failing to properly handle a loaded weapon, and making inappropriate videos, to name a few. Failure or negligence to enforce proper safety training to assure that safety regulations are followed can result in a death knell to a Commander's career.

All this was on my mind as I stepped into the pulpit the next Sunday morning. Chaplain Jay had just commented that Colonel Schreiver was sitting next to his wife in the second row. My message could affect my own career. But I had already decided that I would honor God above honoring man. God had shown me that my prayers were efficacious toward the ends for which I'd prayed. But prayers are sometimes trumped by other principles, if not observed, that may undermine His will.

After I gave the morning's message, I closed saying, "God holds the leadership of this post responsible for everything that happens on it." I noted how the Post Commander's ears reddened as he scowled back at me.

"God is not pleased when leadership makes decisions that condone immorality, cause dissension and divorces in marriages. Such evil decisions mitigate against God's favor, His blessings, and His protection.

Furthermore, the Officers' Club is colluding with evil by bringing young German women from off post to strip in front of Soldiers for the sake of profit. It is shameful, abusive to women and prejudicial to good order and discipline."

I called on every Christian in the chapel to pray for God to bring change.

Ungodly leadership can sometimes remove godly protection. The congregation knew the person responsible—the Post Commander, seated in the chapel next to his wife. The officers wives' prayer group had prayed for months that God would stop this activity. From the corner of my eye, I spotted Colonel Schreiver's wife poke her husband in the ribs with her elbow and lean over to whisper something. As you might expect, he was not happy.

"Does the Word of God speak to us today?"

It certainly did that morning.

After the service I stood at the chapel door shaking hands with those leaving. The Post Commander spoke a word to Chaplain Jay, avoiding me as if I were invisible. The officers' wives were supportive of my sermon and it appeared that godly conviction was settling in on some of their Army husbands.

Later that Sunday I received a phone call from Chaplain Jay. He said:

"Dixey, Colonel Schreiver ordered me to never let any visiting chaplain speak in chapel *ever* again. Colonel Schreiver wants you in his office, promptly, at zero nine hundred tomorrow morning."

Everything on an Army Post belongs to the Post Commander, including the chaplain and the post chapel.

Chaplains have to walk a fine line between base policies, politics, and God's instructions. Are chaplains on the base to offer a prophetic voice to the community and the Commander? Are we to proclaim the whole gospel, or speak with political correctness? Every chaplain must decide how he/she will conduct services and his/her career. In retrospect, I could have taken an alternate course of action, but would that have changed anything?

I had to report this approaching meeting to my own Battalion Commander, so that he would not get blindsided. Lieutenant Colonel McDonald told me, "Dixey, no matter what Colonel Schreiver says, you are good to go in my book. Whatever happens, don't worry about it. Even though he does outrank me, I don't think too much will come of it. You're under my command, not his. You are on the right side."

LTC McDonald's words brought me great relief as I braced myself for the Monday morning appointment. Upon entering Colonel Schreiver's office at 0900, he was seated in front of his array of eagle statues, awards and glass-framed command colors. I stood in front of him, rendering salute, "Chaplain Behnken reporting as ordered, Sir!" He responded with, "At ease; have a seat chaplain."

I considered this might not go as bad as I had anticipated as he could have left me standing at attention, holding my salute the entire time.

"Chaplain, have you heard of the Big Cheese before?"

I replied, "Yes, Sir."

"Well, let's just get this straight. I am the Big Cheese on this post. I call the shots. Do you get that, chaplain?"

I said, "Yes, Sir." He went on to say that his wife had nagged him for months to stop bringing strippers to the Officers' Club. He conceded that it was not the most moral thing to do, but there were worse things, like *poor morale* in the command climate on his OER rating.

"Sir," I said, "if one of those girls was your daughter, would you want her out there stripping in front of those men?" He glanced down, not answering. "That's all, chaplain. Just remember who the Big Cheese is." Later, Chaplain Jay called me after his staff meeting: "Thanks to you, Dixey, the Post Commander just changed the policy at the Officers' Club. No more strippers."

31

The Mountain Surrendered (St Johann, Austria)

BRIAN BRACELIN, AN ARMY Specialist and a great friend of our kids and family, drove into the driveway at our home in Kützburg, Germany. He would stay with our kids while Julie and I made a four-day ski trip to Kitzbühel, Austria, home to the famous World Cup Downhill Slalom Race in the Austrian Alps. We envisioned the exquisite snow-laden chalet scene in the town of Kirchberg im Tyrol.

Julie and I loved skiing together since I taught her in the Alps surrounding Berchtesgaden, Germany, some 15 years earlier. Our French made LeCar Renault took us over a snowy five-hour autobahn drive. We had skied the Tirolean Alps only once before. We loved skiing the mountain range of 51 ski lifts which serviced an uphill capacity of 91,000 riders per hour, over its 170 kilometers (102 square miles) of freshly groomed snow. Only one thing could spoil our dream.

But we would not realize it until the end of the first day of skiing. We climbed onto the 50-passenger gondola to ascend the 15,000-foot mountains then revisited our most favorite sites, like stopping for goulash soup and Glühwein in small restaurants dotting the ski slopes. Every morning two to eight inches of freshly fallen powder snow covered the entire area of ski trails.

After an exquisite day skiing 20 miles of trails, we left the slopes feeling the delightful fatigue of the rigorous exercise. At the end of the trail, a ski bus took us back to our car. When I reached into my pocket for the keys … my heart sank. I checked all my pockets and finally announced "Julie, the keys are missing; did I give them to you?"

She checked, then sadly shook her head; a shadow crept over the remainder of the evening. *How would we drive back to the hotel and then back home to Germany?*

Breaking into the car and hot-wiring would have been an option except for the steering wheel lock that would not allow me to turn the wheel, even if I did get it started. I know because I spent the next two hours finding that out the hard way!

We hailed a taxi to take us to our hotel. The following morning, we decided to retrace our 20 miles of skiing on the same ski lift areas. I told a fellow Austrian skier on the Hahnenkammbahn gondola about our demise; his remark stung me. "If the mountain has your keys, the mountain will keep your keys."

We hoped that we would prove his words wrong. I had the strategy of asking every restaurant and bungalow manager if someone had turned in our keys to their "lost and found." At every ski lift I would ask the loading assistant if someone had turned the keys in. I recalled falling three times the previous day. *Maybe if we thoroughly cover the spots where I fell, the keys will glitter through the snow in the sunlight.*

Knowing that tons of snow are pushed over the previous skiers' paths by each passing skier and that three inches of new snow had fallen, didn't boost our chances. After searching three hours and checking the restaurants along the way and at least 15 ski lift operators, nothing had turned up.

As we skied, I prayed, *Lord, maybe if someone falls near where I fell, they will happen to see my keys and turn them in?*

I spotted a sunken body impression left in the snow where I fell the day before. We searched the area thoroughly but found nothing. *Is this a useless idea?*

At the bottom of the mountain, when we climbed onto the next chairlift, I was distracted and tired; I forgot to ask this operator for the keys.

Julie said: "Dixey, you forgot to ask!"

We were about 20-feet above the ground already when I turned back and yelled, "*Hat jemand einege Autoschlüssel gefunden*?" (Has anyone found a set of auto keys?)

The operator reached into his pocket, held up a set of keys, smiled and yelled back, "*Vielleicht diesen?*" (Perhaps these?) When I saw they were ours, I shouted, "*Alleluia! Wir kommen gleichzeitig zurück!*" (We're coming right back!)

We delightfully retrieved our keys and skied the slopes with joy the remainder of the day. The chance of finding lost keys on top of an Alpine range is quite remote. How much does prayer have to do with it? The mountain did surrender.

In II Kings 6:1-7, a worker begged the prophet Elisha to retrieve a lost axe head that flew off his handle into a lake. Elisha prayed, threw a stick into the lake and the axe head floated up. Some would say that lost keys are too small an issue to merit God's miraculous involvement in our lives. I'd beg to differ as I drove our car home that evening still married.

32

Wave upon Waves of Mercy

IN MY OFFICE, A WIFE, Mary, told me she had witnessed a thorough turnaround (an absolute conversion) in her husband's life in the last few weeks resulting from the counseling he had been doing with me. He went from being the most outrageous, sometimes devilish, angry person, to the kindest God-loving, gentle husband in such a short time.

Mary had purchased tickets earlier to take her children and fly home to the states; she was ready to call it quits. But, I asked her to stay and give me just two weeks to work with her husband, Michael before actually leaving. She decided to wait and give me the time.

His change was so pronounced that the entire battalion knew he somehow how changed. Mary said, "I don't know what you did for my husband, but could you help me find Jesus the same way you helped Michael? "I want a relationship with God too.

"Of course!" I led Mary in praying the simple prayer that I prayed when I first invited Jesus to come into my life, and that I taught her husband. While Michael had received much healing and deliverance from his past, Mary prayed to receive Christ and I shared with her how to grow in her faith.

I told her to start reading the gospel of John. I suggested that she might want to share with her husband the decision which she had just made.

"Chaplain," Mary said, "now, we can have a Christ honoring marriage, and our kids will grow up loving the Lord too!"

Their lives were so changed that they requested a renewal of vow's ceremony and wanted to invite their friends. A ripple effect began to course through their friends' marriages where other couples wanted to have Christ in the center of their lives as well. Another couple asked if I would also do a renewal of vow's ceremony for them.

Michael began bringing his Soldiers in to see me. They too, came to a relationship with Jesus, creator of the universe. For the next year, the move of the Holy Spirit which started in the life of one Soldier continued to move other Soldiers along with their wives and families in the battalion, bringing them closer to Jesus. Michael's testimony even affected a chaplain across the office from me who worked in our sister Armor Battalion. That Chaplain asked me to pray with him too.

"Dixey," he said, "I have watched you ever since you came here two years ago. You have been through some of the most incredible circumstances and experiences I have ever seen or heard. Your faith impresses me. When I first got assigned here, I really did not believe that there was any such thing as *personal evil.* But now having lived here, I have seen real evil in so many personal ways; it boggles my mind. I feel like I have only known *about* Jesus, Dixey, whereas you seem to truly *know* Him. Could you pray with me and help me to know Jesus the way you know Him?" We bowed our heads.

At a Soldier's prayer breakfast that about 80 of the Soldiers attended from my battalion, Michael gave his testimony. He got back up at the end and announced before all that he asked my forgiveness for commandeering the Chaplain's vehicle and painting a playboy silhouette on its roof. The crowd had a good laugh and it became the talk of the post. More Soldiers and families continued to join the chapel.

* * *

Following these good tidings, another blessing came our way. Thirteen years after our venture of faith launching the Anastasis ship ministry in Venice with YWAM, I heard that the ship would spend a month in port to re-provision supplies in Hamburg.

As chaplain, I developed a Spiritual Formation Retreat and took 10 of my Schweinfurt Soldiers to Hamburg, Germany for a two-week volunteer work camp on the Anastasis Ship. It was loading medical and humanitarian supplies for its next mission to flooded Poland. Seeing Don Stephens and the Anastasis crew of 400 changing the world through faith and human aid challenged us all. Don warmly welcomed us aboard ship. We rejoiced in God's faithfulness together! The greater the vision, the longer it takes to get the vision off the ground. Don's vision still lives and grows today. Our seed gift of $1,000 plus the gifts of thousands more helped to create this ministry. It was quite miraculous how God provided the growth.

* * *

The thought I had 17 years before about doing genealogical research and connecting with Behnken relatives began to grow in my heart. I discovered 64 Behnken families in the Bremen area.

After writing each family, sadly, only five returned a response. All five families said they were sorry, but we are not related. Then, one final letter came which proved to be from a second cousin to my great-grandfather, Herman Matthias Behnken.

This cousin called me, speaking broken English. "My name is Jürgen Behnken. I'm from the suburb of Walle. Sonja and I would love to have you come and stay in our home for a few days so we can get to know each other." My spirit soared.

Another dream realized. We drove to Bremen, met and became friends!

A few years later, he and his wife, Sonja, eventually came to my parent's home in Brookville, Ohio and attended an American Behnken Reunion. Jürgen dazzled the crowd with his accordion playing skills. Jürgen found he was not related to the other 63 German families as far as he could investigate from the Bremen City Archive's records of the last two centuries. The Ohio Behnkens were his only living relatives!

To celebrate, we toasted our re-connection with Jäegermeißter, which translates as *Hunting Master.* Jäegermeißter is a sweet decadent blackberry liqueur, 70 proof. The slogan attending the toast is: "Rot wie die Liebe" (Red like love). The "hunt" for the German Behnken tribe was over and we were filled with the "love" of family heritage. This felt like a miracle; and no, I wasn't drunk.

33

Congressional Favor

ONE OF THE MAJOR points in an Army Chaplain's career is choosing a career specialty. I desperately wanted to win selection to become a Family Life Chaplain (FLC) as I loved helping families and young married couples build stronger relationships. At this time of my career, I had to choose one of five options.

The FLC training option offered a high reward, a second Master's Degree. After receiving training, the FLC trains new chaplains in counseling skills, supervises them and directs family life programs for the entire post for three years.

Among the approximately 750 active-duty Army Captain ranking chaplains, only five are chosen each year before the selection board to receive the Special Designator (76K) as FLC. An additional two chaplains are selected on a standby list for contingencies. The opportunity only comes once.

Through the end of 1989 and beginning of 1990, I applied through normal channels for the FLC training which demanded piles of top academic credentials, references from supervisory chaplains and my Officer Evaluation Reports.

Competition with other chaplains for this slot was tight. I hoped my Magna Cum Laude seminary distinction helped tip the scales, but still, this would not be a slam dunk. The list came out while I was in the field training. My name did not make the list of five.

I prayed, *Oh Lord, I believe this is what I am called to do in my career.* When you don't make the list of five, your name is normally placed on the list for attending Hospital Chaplain Training or Clinical Pastoral Education (CPE) – not my first areas of interest.

A month later I received notice while training in Grafenwoehr that Congress had just appropriated funding for two more FLCs to study this year.

My name appeared on the secondary list to go! WOW!

Within weeks, orders were cut and presented to me. I actually held paperwork that would cover all expenses (well over $100,000) for a Master's Degree in Marriage, Family and Community Development at the University of Maryland, College Park.

The only caveat was that the two-year Master's program must be crammed into 18 months. I had to move from Schweinfurt, Germany to Fort

Monmouth, New Jersey for six months of Advanced Chaplain training and go on to the University of Maryland, Washington, D.C. area within two weeks following the Advanced course.

Three days before our flight to the States as Julie and I prepared to move to the east coast, the war brewing in Iraq challenged all our plans. *Immediate cancellation of all leaves and travel orders* came down through 1st Brigade. My unit received orders to ship to Iraq.

We had to stay in Schweinfurt and I had to go to war instead.

After all the work we had done in preparation to move, our rotation to the States stopped in its tracks. I would now miss the FLC training at the University of Maryland.

We prayed, *Lord, our household goods and car are already on a ship to the States. We have vacated our rented German quarters and turned in the keys, now living in the guesthouse on post awaiting our flight. What will my family do now if I have to go to war? I'll be gone for at least a year. Can You intercede for us? Amen."*

* * *

Two days later, a Pentagon FAX arrived for me through USAREUR and down through Division. *"Proceed as ordered to attend training at University of Maryland."* The Army decided that my career progression preempted all other orders, even war. Within three days, we arrived in Fort Monmouth, New Jersey to pursue God's next journey for our lives. That news came as a great relief. Our hearts overflowed at God's undeserved favor.

"Praise the LORD, my soul, and forget not all his benefits—[3] who forgives all your sins and heals all your diseases, [4] who redeems your life from the pit and crowns you with love and compassion, [5] who satisfies your desires with good things so that your youth is renewed like the eagle's." Psalm 103:2-5 (NIV).

God moves in mysterious ways, his wonders to perform.

34

Miracles Need Working Out

AFTER OUR SIX MONTHS at the Chaplain's Advanced Course, my next hurdle became getting the University of Maryland to approve a curriculum for an 18-month study to obtain my second Master's Degree. The required two-year program which they already described was intense. No one had ever completed all the courses, labs, and therapy supervision hours in such a short time frame at University of Maryland.

God again provided a mentor, Chaplain (MAJ) Janet Horton, a gifted administrator who worked at the Pentagon Chief of Chaplain's office mentored me through the maze of academic juggernauts. Her mettle, brilliance and determination seeded her 10 years later to become the first female chaplain (Colonel) in a Combat Division in American history. God also opened up a clinical supervision opportunity at Fort Meade under the guidance of a certified American Association of Marriage and Family Therapy (AAMFT) Clinical Supervisor, Chaplain (LTC) Richard Thompson.

Little did I realize that this program of study would demand six days a week from 5 a.m. to midnight for the next year and a half. Julie tirelessly cared for our four children by herself, almost experiencing the life of a single mother. I am deeply thankful for her loyalty and fortitude. Julie's unmitigated commitment got me through.

My course of studies led to serving eventually in two three-year tours as a Family Life Chaplain training chaplains and receiving my clinical associate membership in the AAMFT in Fort Leonard Wood, Missouri and Fort Clayton, Republic of Panama for the next seven years.

God had heard my prayer, moved the U.S. Congress to act on my behalf, preempted my war orders, changed a university dictate, and sent chaplains to help me walk through the academic maze. His faithfulness endures to all generations. All of these seemed impossible from the onset, yet the impossible became possible. HOOAH!

35

Divine Protection in Iraq?

FOLLOWING OUR ASSIGNMENT at Fort Sill (June 1999-May 2002), we moved to Yuma Proving Grounds (YPG), Arizona where I became the Post Chaplain after finishing the Division Chaplains' Course at Fort Jackson, South Carolina. Toward the end of our time at YPG, the Iraqi War began escalating. I wondered *again*, if I would be going.

I soon heard through the grapevine that my new orders would take us to Darmstadt, Germany to the 22nd Signal Brigade. The new unit already knew their rotation to Iraq was slated, but I had to keep it under wraps.

By now, our oldest daughter, Rachael had married and become a missionary in Brazil. Lukas went to Hollywood to become an actor and Hope had just graduated college and moved to Hollywood to become a musician. Brandon joined us in our return to Germany. He wanted to hitchhike through Europe.

We moved for the fourth time back to Germany. This time I knew I would be going to war. Robin Williams played the character of AFN Radio DJ, Adrien Cronauer, in the movie *Good Morning Vietnam!* On his arrival in Vietnam, he saw rows of dead bodies lined up on the tarmac awaiting their flight home. That visual came to mind as I contemplated our duty in Iraq. As all Soldiers do, I wondered if I would march onto a returning plane or return from Iraq inside a box.

What would be my life's final moment?

The two primary questions that I entertained in May of 1971 at the age of 21 when I reported to the draft board during the Vietnam War were: *Will I have to kill anyone?* and *Will I be killed?* The two questions from 35 years before were reduced to only one question since I now served as a *non-combatant* chaplain.

Official orders to the 22nd Signal Brigade, V Corps, arrived and we prepared for our move in February 2005. The transition went smoothly. After we settled into our new housing in Lincoln Village, Darmstadt, our 11 years of living in this country made us feel right at home.

Julie would be living here without me as did all the other wives for a full year once our unit shipped out. Brandon David stopped in from time to time between his travels across Europe.

Our unit had one game plan, *Get Ready!* It demanded many preparatory deployments prior to shipping off that would take me away most of the six months preceding October 6th, 2005. As part of Task Force Adler, Iraq, I would train and supervise seven Battalion Chaplains composed of some 2,500 Soldiers, male and female.

We would become the AT&T of Iraq for four communication nets: U.S. Forces, NIPR (Non-classified Internet Protocol) and SIPR (Secure Internet Protocol) network, Coalition Forces, and our newly trained Iraqi Forces net.

This task also required hundreds of civilian contractors under our protection over the 168,000 square miles of Iraq. Every base needed Communications.

The three pillars of Army doctrine of "*shoot, move, communicate*" have never changed.

While in Grafenwoehr, two weeks before departure to Iraq, I came to an emotional equilibrium about the 'Will I be killed?' issue.

I could live in fear of death, or, I could put the fear of death to rest by reconciling myself to the fact that I can *give up* my right to live, to God. After much struggle, I resolved to let it go and not battle with it anymore. I handed my life over to the Lord in prayer and emotionally released any power I thought I had to the One who has all power. Since that day, I've felt a new freedom from my concern.

This book's cover photo captures our departing group prayer before leaving Darmstadt. Our Soldiers and family members kneeled on the street in front of our headquarters, joining Julie and me in prayer for our safe deployment and return. We prayed for Soldiers assigned to Task Force Adler, deployed from several German and U.S. Bases to Camp Victory, Baghdad, Balad, Tikrit, Mosul and others. And, we prayed that our families remaining home in our absence would be cared for and protected.

While based in Camp Victory, I pastored the evening worship service held in Saddam's former hunting lodge. One of my greatest privileges was baptizing one of our Muslim translators code-named *Raven* and seven other Soldiers in Saddam's swimming pool near the Al Faw palace.

When our one-year tour ended, we found that God answered our prayer of protection for our troop's safety over the hundreds of thousands of miles traveled in convoys throughout the year in a marvelous way! To be sure, there were injuries from IEDs, VBIEDs, mortars, rockets and gunfire, but not one Soldier lost a limb, eyesight, hearing or life. Every Soldier that deployed with us returned home!

Brigadier General Dennis Via, Commander of Fifth Signal Command, stated at the Uncasing of the Colors Ceremony on our homecoming back to Darmstadt, that this feat was nothing less than a miracle.

While we have been blessed with so many of God's miracles, we also lived through struggles, pain and disappointment.

Three weeks after my return from Iraq to Germany, my parents suffered a tragic car accident in Florida which resulted in both of them losing their lives due to accident-related injuries. As executor of their estate and related collateral issues, I felt it necessary to take an elective early retirement from the Army with over 23 years of active duty as a chaplain.

36

Recall to Active Duty

AFTER DEALING WITH THE legal matters of my parents' estate, Julie and I purchased an old seaworthy 26-foot 1970 Columbia sailboat to live on while in Los Angeles and spent time with two of our adult children there.

With time, we healed from our losses, and learned to sail, which had always been Julie's dream. Over the next eight months, we took three ASA certified sailing courses, joined the Hurricane Gulch Yacht Club at Cabrillo Marina, San Pedro and sailed over a thousand miles around the California Coasts and the Channel Islands. Our greatest test was the Gale force winds we encountered returning from Catalina Island one day fighting 10-foot seas for 6 hours.

To top it off, our hearts grew so fond of sailing the deep blue that we flew to Hawaii and joined a crew of three to help sail a 55-foot Dutch Trintella Cutter to San Diego. The sail took 21 days to go 3,000 miles. That story will be told another day.

Due to the urgent family demands that surrounded my hasty elective retirement from the Army, I began longing and dreaming of returning to the chaplaincy. But could I ever get back into the Army? In my entire chaplain career, I had never heard of a chaplain getting a recall to active duty. The only chaplains I knew serving beyond the Mandatory Retirement Date (MRD), age 62, were Roman Catholic priests and Flag Officers, the Chief and Deputy Chief of Chaplains.

Once, I met a previously retired Catholic priest, age 68, on a special contract with the chaplaincy due to the fact that the Army chaplaincy faced a 30% deficit of Roman Catholic priests to fill their quota. The Army must try to uphold a representative percentage demographic of the societal levels of religious denominations. But if there are not enough chaplain applicants to fill the slots because the Catholic church cannot supply enough, then a mandatory retired Catholic priest may be re-contracted annually to serve until they are medically unable to serve.

Certainly, I couldn't become a Catholic priest to get back in, but a thought struck me. I wondered if having a chaplain specialty, Family Life Chaplain, that the Army needs would qualify me for *special contract provisions* that are made for Catholic priests? I had never heard of an FLC or a Protestant chaplain getting recalled to active duty, but it was worth looking into.

In the Army, every officer branch has a special designator number. One for Infantry, one for Artillery, one for chaplains and so forth. The Special 'K' designation is placed behind my chaplain designator of 76. Thus, 76K is marked on my records for receiving an Army directed Master's Degree for FLC training in 'Marriage and Family Counseling'.

I called my good friend of 20 years, Chaplain (Colonel) Jim Agnew, Deputy FORSCOM Chaplain, and asked if the chaplaincy had any vacancies that needed filling for FLCs. And is it possible to come back in for a three-year tour contract in a 76K deficit slot? He had never heard of that before but would check into it.

The FORSCOM Personnel Chaplain worked across the hall from Jim and I heard him call a chaplain's name in the next office and pose the question to him. That chaplain said he'd call the Pentagon and get an answer.

The next day, Chaplain Agnew called me. He shared enthusiastically,

"Dixey, if this is what you really want to do, we can make it happen! It will take 90 days to run your National Security Check and get all the proper paperwork in order. Once cleared, we can have orders in your hands in 30 days. Do you want to go to Grafenwoehr, Germany; Stuttgart, Germany; Hohenfels, Germany; Fort Knox, Kentucky or Fort Polk, Louisiana?"

Since I had been stationed in Germany three times already, and that would mean separation from Julie six months at a time, I did not want Germany. I was stationed at Fort Knox for my MOS training in 1971, so I elected to go to Fort Polk, a place I had never been. This meant I would be living 900 miles away from Julie and our new condo home we purchased in Sarasota, FL. for three years. We had been separated during my career for three years already. We knew our marriage could stand the test of time to secure our retirement dreams, a home on the water, and a yacht we could see from our back balcony. I sent in the paperwork.

I planned on traveling home for one week every three months for leave. Meanwhile, Julie set her sights on renovating our condo unit and securing the purchase of a 1991 32-foot *Island Packet.* Peter, the condo owner who owned the yacht named *Morning Grace*, was asking way too much for it; his exorbitant figure did not fit into our budget. We would wait, hoping the price would go down.

When the Army called from the retirement section, my orders said: *Report to Fort Jackson, SC for two weeks of Re-integration Training on June 21, 2009, then proceed to Fort Polk, LA. as Director of the Family Life Chaplain and Ministries Training Center.* That's funny, I entered the Army the first time under less than voluntary conditions on June 21, 1971. Now, 39 years later, I would serve three more years after retiring at my own request. People have often told me, *be careful what you ask for, you may just get it.* Julie and I had our goals before us. We both prayed they would eventually work out.

One of the sweet spots of living the life of faith is that you never know what's going to happen. Some would call it a capricious lifestyle. Turns out, we were suited for the adventurous lifestyle.

As I entered the reporting office in Fort Jackson, I recognized a man I once knew as a Major, CH David Willett, a Catholic priest. He looked up at me with such a shock of recognition that our first response was to hug rather than salute. He was a Colonel now, and I, a Lieutenant Colonel. David was my first chaplain boss in Schweinfurt, Germany back in 1987, when I was a young Captain. He requested recall back to active-duty chaplaincy for three more years – just as I had. For the next two weeks after our re-orientation training, we spent many evenings recalling former times.

Best I knew, I was the only Protestant FLC ever recalled to active duty. Another miracle?

There may be others I don't know about, possibly for war-time buildup. But I'd never heard of them and the idea was novel to everyone I spoke to. I queried if God had planned all of these meetings with old acquaintances and new ones, or was it just a series of coincidences?

Leaving orientation in Fort Jackson, South Carolina, I wondered what working under Chaplain (COL) David Darbyshire would be like in Fort Polk. I knew David from my time in Europe when he was the USAREUR Chaplain Command Personnel Director in 2008.

37

Looking for Affordable Rent

WHEN I ARRIVED AT the Holiday Inn Express in Leesville near Fort Polk, I prayed, *Lord, please direct me to a place to live that will not be too costly.* I planned on buying a Fifth Wheel RV Trailer and living in a trailer park, near base. Then, after three years I'd resell the RV for virtually the same price I paid for it. The going rate for a small one-bedroom rental apartment and utilities was $1,000 a month. If I could lower the rent, I could save roughly $30,000 over the next three years to help buy *Morning Grace.*

The next morning, I asked the young local lady serving fried catfish and black-eyed peas for breakfast if there were any trailer parks on a lake near the base that she knew about. *Well, darling, it so hap'ns that my Uncle Winston on my mama's side, twice removed, is the manager of a tral'r park on Anacoco Lake. Bout tin miles from heeer—he takes in anyone need'n a place.*

My heart warmed. When she smiled, two black holes greeted me from where her teeth used to be. I wondered what I might be getting myself into.

I headed to the VFW landing. After deciding which of the three RVs I'd seen to buy the night before on Craigslist, I wound my way around and up and down the thickly wooded pine forests along the backroads.

I asked a young thin fella at the trailer Park with a glove on his left hand that hung limp at his side, "Is Winston here?" Just looking at this wiry young man kind of unnerved me. He introduced himself as Bobby, Winston's son. He had some missing teeth too. Then I said, "I'm looking for a slab to hook up my RV – do you have a vacancy?" He replied, "You want my dad, he's over in the bait shack."

I left Bobby under the makeshift kitchen hut and walked across the concrete patio that led to a bait house/home where two old leaky roof trailers had been fastened together with aluminum siding and lag bolts. A corrugated aluminum roof stood above it to keep out the rain. I spotted Winston through the screen door and knocked.

A soft-spoken older gentleman whose face betrayed some rough times, met me at the door. I gathered from his backwoods Louisiana drawl, that I could have a place with a great view of the lake for $100 a month and that water and sewer were free.

Electric would be $25-$30 a month depending on how much I use. Everyone gets a ten-day grace period if they can't get enough funds together by the first day of the month. I took the spot, gave Winston my deposit plus a month's rent and left to purchase a 26-foot fifth wheeler RV. It would be the first RV trailer I'd ever lived in.

With job secured, home set up, new neighbors to meet and a new office to unpack, my days at Fort Polk unfolded. It wasn't until a week after I'd moved into my fifth wheel trailer at the VFW landing that I discovered Winston was a felon. He told me he'd murdered his son-in-law in cold blood a few years before, right in front of his daughter in a bar with the shotgun he kept stowed in the back window of his truck. He'd warned the boy never to beat his daughter again. But the kid just didn't listen.

A few weeks later, I discovered we had other felons living on the property: a blind lady who lived alone, a mother-daughter prostitution ring, a drug dealer, a mentally ill teenager, a registered female sex predator with an ankle-tracking bracelet and a host of other troubled characters. Winston had a soft heart for felons and others, like himself.

My three years at Fort Polk were immensely full and rewarding. The Post Chaplain, (COL) David Darbyshire and I hit it off extremely well. I ran the Family Life Center from the Main Post Chapel office and often filled in for David at the General's staff meetings.

At the beginning of my second year at Polk, when CH Darbyshire retired, CH David Waters came into my office. I knew him. David came seeking me for an interview some 25 years earlier at Fort Bragg – my first duty assignment, to gain endorsement with my denomination. I'd seen him at the CFGC annual conference once a year ever since.

"David Waters!" I said, pointing to his eagle rank (Colonel's) on his uniform. "Correction, I mean, SIR! Great to see you again!"

"Dixey Behnken! Guess what? I'm your new boss."

I smiled and he smiled as we bear-hugged. David, now a full Colonel, had been promoted as the new Fort Polk Post Chaplain. I would serve with him for a full year.

Over the next 2 years, I counseled many Soldiers returning from Afghanistan recovering from severe PTSD through EMDR psychotherapy and ran family enrichment and couples communication retreats.

God also moved mightily upon a number of the people that I lived among at the Anacoco trailer camp, becoming friends with most of them. I've always felt that friendship evangelism is the best way to touch people's lives.

Toward the end of my duty there, Bobby, with the limp arm, asked me to marry him and Sharon – the blind lady. They asked me if they could sing: *"In heaven there ain't no beer, that's why we drink it here,"* as the closing wedding song.

The following Saturday, we celebrated the wedding, dancing with them on the concrete patio next to the bait house. Turns out, they never sang it, they'd just said that to tease me to see if I'd still marry them. Later, the next day, we had boiled crawfish. I'd never eaten it before and I said, "Sharon, show me how you eat this!" She said, *"Ya peel the tail, and bite the head off, like this."* I followed her lead and ate my first crawfish.

Bobby called me six months after I left Ft. Polk to say he received Christ as his Lord and Savior. Joan, the prostitute, felt God's touch and healing from her shame and prayed to receive forgiveness. God made that time of my life one of the most unbelievable series of daily surprises I'd ever experienced.

38

Your Boat is Sinking!

TOWARD THE LAST SIX months of my Fort Polk three-year commitment, I began to get serious about buying *Morning Grace.* She still sat in the slip behind our condo and had not sold, even after Peter dropped the price three times. It had been sitting in dock for a year at $59K and Peter had to move. He could not leave the boat behind occupying a condo slip.

After making my 10th 900-mile trip home to Sarasota every three months to spend a week with Julie, we had sailed with Peter twice. The boat seemed seaworthy, although without a marine survey, we could not know for sure. Should we take a gamble and just make an offer? I had a certain price in my head.

The two-foot diameter hole in the fiberglass from a piling that Hurricane Charlie had driven through the front right bow and up through the center ceiling of the front cabin had been properly repaired. But the ceiling part was not done perfectly; I'd have to do more repairs on it. Should I rule out buying the boat altogether?

Julie loved the boat and buying it would save all the time and trouble of finding, inspecting, surveying, purchasing and sailing a boat to Siesta Key from a distant state. We felt a peace about purchasing it since both of our trial sails on her went so smoothly. If we'd done our due diligence, we would have gotten a marine survey. Peter countered my offer and we got a loan before my *Return to Retirement* orders came.

Sanding and repainting the badly weathered teak trim and decor on the boat is something Julie would do until I returned. The next time I came home, it was radiant and looked almost new, despite her 24 years at sea. My friend, Thor, an experienced sailor of over 50 years from Norway, owned a 29-foot *Island Packet* and agreed to inspect our boat with a fine-toothed comb. The seven-page gig sheet he accumulated on a legal sized tablet boggled my mind. I didn't even know what half of the nautical terms meant.

He said "Some of these repairs will be quite costly. I will spare you all the details except for one. *Your boat is sinking!* The packing gland is leaking. Get a True North Marine mechanic here today, now! If power goes out and the batteries die, your boat will be on the bottom!" I thought *what's a packing gland?*

I regretted not getting a marine survey before we bought it. (It's like getting a home inspection before you buy a house). Sometimes you make decisions you come to regret, even when you think you are following the Lord the best you can. I wondered if our purchase was such a great idea after all. What good could come from this?

The mechanic came and fixed the problem in two hours.

After returning to Fort Polk, I completed my third contract year and went home to Sarasota … retired again. My RV sold for a decent price and I closed the final phase of my military career. I looked forward to a couple of years of respite in retirement again and fulfilling Julie's dream. "If we don't do it now, we will be too old later," I thought.

Wondering whether it was wise to pursue a dream that seemed to be strictly for personal pleasure, I pondered if I was squandering our time for self-aggrandizement?

Why would God give us such vast dreams?

Everyone must answer for themselves how spiritual values compete with these kinds of secular appearing first world matters. But deep within I also felt a certain destiny shaping. Perhaps, right now was just a holding pattern for things to fall into place. The question of what the future held confronted me each day.

What does God do with a retired Army chaplain?

39

A Book Changes My Life

THE PHONE RANG. MY son, Lukas, was calling. "Hey dad, are you sitting down?"

"No, I'm not." I found the couch. "I am now!"

"You're not going to believe this! An investor hired me to fly to Africa, to Kenya, to shoot my very first movie!"

His voice betrayed the anticipation of the culmination of intense years of hard work. Both joy and fear swept over me. I was glad I'd sat down.

Lukas had been a struggling actor for 15 years with TV roles as a guest actor, commercials and Class B movies. After developing a greater interest in producing and with his many years of experience acting, this would be his first shot at a full-feature documentary movie, with his newly formed company, *Sterling Light Productions.*

"That's fabulous!" I shouted. "When are you going?"

"Not sure yet, probably two or three months."

I took a deep breath. All I could think about was the Nairobi Westgate shopping mall massacre five months before by four masked Muslim gunmen – it still haunted me. Over 70 died and several hundreds were wounded. *Did Lukas remember this?* I wondered but didn't dare speak of it and destroy his excitement with my fears.

"Tell me about it." I asked.

"Have you ever heard of Charles Mulli?"

"No, I've never heard of him."

"Okay Dad, let me read you the film caption."

"It will tell what happens when a six-year-old boy in Kenya is abandoned by his family and left to raise himself on the streets. MULLY is no ordinary rags-to-riches tale. It's the true story of Charles Mully, whose unlikely stratospheric rise to wealth and power leaves him questioning his own existence, searching for meaning in life. Against the better judgment of family and community, MULLY sets out to enrich the fate of over 8,000 orphaned children across Kenya. Jeopardizing his own life and the security of his family, Charles Mully risks everything and sets in motion a series of events that is nothing short of astonishing."

"The movie will be a documentary-drama. Dad, get the book: *Father to the Fatherless*, by Paul Boge and read his story. It's unbelievable – you are going to love it. Oh! I have to hop off, my executive producer is calling." (It's a rare phone call when we are not interrupted by someone else demanding his immediate attention.)

I took a notepad and wrote down the name, Charles Mulli.

NOTE: {Charles spells his name two ways: "Mulli," is his personal family name and for tax purposes he spells it "Mully" to separate his business ventures and Mully Children's Family (MCF) organization}.

* * *

"Great work, son, I'm so proud of you!"

After purchasing the book on Amazon, I settled down to read it. The same deep emotions of compassion stirred within, compelling and overwhelming me, like the first time I started supporting an orphan some 43 years before.

I thought about my future, not quite knowing what I wanted to do after my second retirement, besides making Julie's dreams of sailing come true. An Army Chaplain's job doesn't easily translate to church pastor. I wasn't sure I wanted all the politics, committee meetings and fundraising which come with running a church. But now, the thought of helping orphans in a greater way intrigued me.

The idea had always interested me but had never materialized. Maybe this would reveal God's direction for my future? When I finished the book, I felt a deep inner urging: "*Buy a round trip ticket to Kenya and meet Charles Mulli.*"

"Is that you, God?" I whispered audibly.

I have heard that inner voice so strongly only a few times in my life. I began researching the web for travel alerts on recent Muslim terrorism in Kenya. Gruesome killings still continued … but now I had to go! The flight ticket would cost over $2,500.

It would take some time to work out all the details.

With the movie rights secured, Scott Haze, the director and Lukas began selecting a film crew of two other men and one woman. They planned on leaving November 2013 through January 2014 for a six-week Phase One shoot. Maybe I could join Lukas during the Phase Two shoot in April/May. Julie considered going with me but her concerns over terrorism held her at bay. She told me this would be a great father/son time together, and besides she had been to Kenya once before on a mission trip.

After praying together, she did not feel God releasing her to go.

My ticket had a two-city stopover as I wanted to take two weeks in Holland on my return trip to visit my other son, Brandon David, who lived in Deventer with his family. Lukas also planned on joining me there.

Through every step of the way, I encouraged Lukas and discovered how to effectively pray for him in this venture. His wife, Katherine, set up a daily 15 minute four-way phone prayer session (which I still have the notes from).

A real provision came through when Lukas needed to rent cameras and movie equipment of all kinds in Los Angeles worth well over $1,000,000 to take with them for both phases. When he told each rental agency about the Mulli story, most wanted to help, generously dropping two-thirds off the normal rental fees. That was major!

Just the logistics of moving 28 large cases of camera equipment through Amsterdam customs stymies my imagination. The film crew would need half a bus or truck just to transport the equipment to and from the airports and to the filming locations in Ndalani, Yatta and Nairobi.

Several things needed to happen before I could join Lukas in Kenya in late April. I needed Dr. Charles Mulli's invitation to come to MCF during the filming, as well as the film director. Furthermore, I had not considered the complexities of arranging for my arrival and stay in a third world nation until I experienced it for myself.

Lukas shared my desire to come with Dr. Mulli throughout the first filming phase. When Lukas called and told me Dr. Mulli and Scott concurred with my visit for the second filming phase. I was elated.

I had seen Lukas acting on many sets but had never seen him in action producing a movie. This would be a double treat for me, meeting Dr. Mulli and observing Lukas make his first movie. I kept pinching myself. My life is vaster than my dreams.

Am I really living this?

With my trip to Africa scheduled five months from now, and the five years of planning we had made for realizing Julie's sailing dream, two matters remained. One, could we find someone to coach us on sailing to the Bahamas; and two, would we be able to sail back in time to catch my flight to Kenya?

It was providential how God connected us to our three-month buddy-boaters who would mentor us on our sail to the Bahamas.

I made a phone call about hooking up electrical connections for a new marine Balmar 70 AMP alternator to the 24 hp Yanmar diesel on the Island Packet owner's website. The gentleman who answered gave me explicit directions. Then I asked him if he knew anyone sailing to the Bahamas in February. Hayden laughed, "Are you reading my mind? My wife, Radeen and I have gone the last three years, and we are heading out of Dinner Key Marina in Miami about Feb. 21st. Do you want to buddy-boat with us?"

We met with Hayden and Radeen Cochran the following week to make plans. We sailed off two months later and ended up spending nine weeks at sea with them, learning the Atlantic tides, weather, Bahamian culture, history, islands and people. It was a very amazing experience and we returned home a week before my flight left for Kenya. I will share those stories another time. It was my prayer and delight to be able to have provided Julie this sailing adventure of a lifetime. It was the least I could do for her supporting me for 30 years in the Army and 40 years of marriage.

40

Meeting Dr. Mulli

I HAD CHECKED THE WORLD Health Organization (WHO) for their medical directives on travel to Kenya. I would only need to take the Malaria pills prior to, during, and after my travel there. My military shots were still up to date since my 2006 Iraqi deployment. The 20-hour flight on KLM Royal Dutch Airlines routed me through Amsterdam to Kenya. Though I have traveled in over 30 foreign nations; this would be my first trip to Africa.

As our 737 aircraft approached Nairobi by night, the line of lights on the airstrip for the approach caught my eyes. We landed and taxied to the terminal. When I saw the baggage transfer cart approach, I went into a state of temporary shock. It was a John Deere tractor pulling a wagon! Never had I seen this before at any commercial airport.

My first introduction to the Kenyan culture of sandal-footed airport workers dressed in shabby shorts and loose muslin shirts tossing our luggage onto a hay wagon was the first of many more culture shocks. My previous exposure to other third world nation airports was limited to Panama, Kuwait and our U.S. military airport in Baghdad. Neither prepared me for this level of poverty.

I descended the boarding stairs shoved up against our aircraft and walked to the baggage claim. Once outside the terminal, I discovered I could not buy anything. I had not purchased Kenyan shillings back in the States before I left. The Exchange Bureau was behind the exit barrier. It did not allow my reentry from the baggage claim without a ticket once I left. I was stuck with American dollars.

After retrieving my luggage and proceeding to locate my ride, I wondered if I'd find them in this mayhem. Then, I spotted a sign in the distance with my name on it, held by a beautiful young lady with immaculately braided long black hair. She introduced herself as Angela and the man next to her as Thomas, our driver, the MCF hospitality team. Thankfully, she handed me some bottled water I wanted to buy earlier but couldn't.

The olive drab green Land Cruiser had large knobby wheels that lifted us higher than most vehicles on the road. Layers of mud caked its wheel wells. The steering wheel was on the right, indicative of the British influence from their rule over Kenya from 1920 - 1963. We loaded my backpack and computer case into the back hatch and Angela took the front seat next to Thomas while directing me to the back seat.

As we began our trip, I noted they both spoke perfect English with a British tweak. Angela navigated for Thomas to take many of the short cuts through the city of Nairobi to avoid traffic.

"Dixey," Angela explained, "Thomas and I were both orphans. Daddy Mulli rescued us from the streets of the slums years ago when we were children. We grew up at Ndalani where we will be taking you. Since he took us in, Daddy continued taking in children. MCF has over 2,500 children now. Once we reach adulthood we become beneficiaries for two years, giving back to MCF to help the younger children.

After that, we can leave or stay on staff. We're on the staff now and receive more children weekly. I'm sorry to inform you that presently Daddy Mulli is away helping with a family emergency for three days, but he told me he's excited to be meeting you soon. He just loves Lukas. In the meantime, Lukas will keep you busy."

"I can only imagine how caring for so many children kept Dr. Mulli on the go," I said. "And how is Lukas?"

"He is filming three scenes at a time. You raised quite an ambitious energetic son!"

"Thank you, could you tell me the time and how long before we get there?"

"It's 11:30 now and being 120 kilometers away, we will reach MCF around 2:30 a.m., in about three hours."

When I figured the math, 75 miles in three hours, that's an average of 25 miles an hour. I wondered what the road conditions would be like.

Angela told me she coordinated the movie filming crew's logistics, transportation, meals and housing. Thomas directed the agriculture and horticulture operations.

Thomas said, "I direct the 600,000 square feet of hydroponic farming and 300 acres of farming that produce French green beans, vegetables and tomatoes which we export to Europe. I hire, train and supervise over 800 local workers to plow, plant, maintain and harvest mostly by hand. Our agricultural production supports approximately 50% of our self-sustainability operations."

Rough roads greeted us as we left Nairobi, the capitol city; our speed rarely exceeded 30 miles an hour. Every 15 miles or so we came upon a queue of stopped traffic, waiting for a police inspection. It was pitch black out.

Suddenly, Thomas put on the breaks.

We faced our first terrorism checkpoint search blockade. The police controlled and intercepted marauding Muslim terrorist's vehicles with primitively nailed stripboards that narrowed the lanes down to one and would flatten a tire if run over. No one dare cross. The police checked everyone's IDs/passports each time and waved us on.

Stopping like this, every ten miles became routine. I wondered if the police recognized the Mully Children's Family sign painted in English Swahili) across the side of our Land Rover and how widely recognized MCF was across Kenya. Roughly 16% (8.52 million) of the 53.3 million population speak English; about 80% speak some English. Both English and Swahili are 'official' languages.

I wondered how well Dr. Mulli was known throughout Kenya, as it didn't appear that we received special favor. I slipped off to sleep intermittently from my long journey. As we turned off the main road, a bumpy tire-rutted muddy road jostled me.

I awoke. Angela said, "We're almost there." As we slowed rounding a sharp corner and passed through a gate, Thomas braked as people began surrounding us playing African drums and tambourines and singing songs in Swahili. Thomas and Angela must have been in on the preplanning. They opened my door.

I saw Lukas and recognized the director, Scott Haze. Several Kenyan film crew and others encircled us singing a Swahili welcome song. My heart overflowed with joy.

Lukas grabbed my luggage and led me up the stairs to one of the guest dorms near the kitchen patio where he'd been living for three months. Weighted protective mosquito nets hung from the ceiling covering the four corners and sides of both beds. At 3 a.m. I fell asleep exhausted from the 30 hours of traveling.

Robust melodious songs from hundreds of singing children burst through my window waking me at 6:30 a.m. I couldn't see them though as our room was surrounded with huge flowering trees. Lukas slept on as I enjoyed the harmonies with their African rhythm. Could anything be closer to heaven? Still tired, I fell back to sleep.

Waking at 10:30 a.m., we took our showers in the primitive private concrete cubicle ensuite and headed to breakfast. I learned that the filming last night went on until my arrival. I couldn't believe they filmed interviews through the night between 3 a.m. to 5 a.m. two or three times a week, interviewing Mulli, his friends, and his children. Most of the time, Lukas and the film crew captured scenes on two sets at once, with some 20 or 30 people preparing the next day's sets. I had arrived for the last two weeks of the filming project. Lukas showed me his production schedules and the story boards. Scenes and stories were time-lined on a very tightly run schedule.

Since meeting Charles Mulli would have to wait for three days, I would spend the days between Thomas' tour of the children's campus and Lukas' filming sets. I still couldn't believe I was actually here. After reading the book *Father to the Fatherless* twice, I would soon meet the man who has saved and raised more children than any man in history; the numbers exceed 18,000 at this writing. Charles is the African *Mother Theresa*. I felt deeply humbled and privileged to be able to meet him.

Thomas took me to see the modern hydroponic farms. Their enormous size overwhelmed me … I could barely take it all in. He showed me the famous 'Jacob's Well' where the miracle of water occurred. When visiting the school classes in session, the children sang to me (sometimes in English), and six or seven students would quote their favorite Bible verses in English by memory. I also saw their library, computer room and medical facility. Children were always smiling. Surreal doesn't begin to describe my emotions.

Finally, on the third night, Lukas called on me at 10:30 p.m. right before bedtime and said Dr. Mulli had just pulled in and wanted to meet me straight away – not wishing to wait until morning. The excitement in his eyes portrayed my own.

Were we destined to meet from birth?

He still wore his shiny three-piece suit and large brimmed black leather Australian cowboy hat. We sat together at an outdoor picnic table, with his wife Esther joining us. A large grin crossed his face as he spoke his first words, "Dixey, I want you to know that I have adopted Lukas as my son. I am his African father, now!"

I felt honored by this proclamation and told him so. I knew Charles could take Lukas to heights of success far beyond my experience level. Just building the massive Ndalani 500-acre farming complex in the sub-Saharan arid climate was just one enterprise which exemplified his genius. As we talked into the night, we both sensed that our God-directed meeting was only the beginning of a much broader long-term relationship. The *Father to the Fatherless* became my brother-in-Christ and my son's African father. What a treat! Our meeting ended with prayer at about 2:00 a.m. My two weeks with Dr. Mulli and Esther in Kenya started a growing relationship that would strengthen over the next six years.

Watching Lukas produce some 20 film scenes with as many as 200 people in a scene created a deep respect for his growth and expertise in the filming industry. I got to witness an unfolding of events which would take Lukas and me in directions never imagined. The years of supporting orphans from Korea, Morocco, Honduras and Guatemala would culminate in adding Kenyans to our extended family. I tell church audiences that in heaven we will have our international family all in one place!

On our flight back home, we stopped over in Amsterdam with my son, Brandon David, and his Dutch wife and my granddaughter, Ayla. That was icing on the cake as I hadn't seen them in over two years. Lukas could only stay with us for three days.

The contrast of Africa's dirt roads and bare footed beggars against Holland's high speed double-decker electric trains and extremely efficient prosperous society, seemed beyond conception.

The miracle of meeting Dr. Mulli became the creative force for writing this book. God plucked me out of Florida when I had no inkling of what my future held, took me to Kenya then brought me back from Africa as an ambassador for Mully Children's Family. When I stepped back on my flight 10 days later at the Schiphol Airport, I wondered, *what's next?* This new role was tailor made for me.

But I didn't feel I could measure up to the responsibility. The grandness of it emotionally resembled the first time I put on a jump suit and leaped out of an airplane at 12,000 feet for a HALO (High Altitude, Low Opening) tandem jump. The wind hitting me in the face at 100 mph, cheeks puffed wide like a squirrel and falling towards the Arizona desert for two miles before the parachute opened, created the same sensory overload like I was on steroids.

41

"We Are Family"—the Benges

ON MY RETURN FROM KENYA, I called Paul Boge in Winnipeg, Canada, the author of *Father to the Fatherless.* He is a nickel mining engineer, an author of nine books, a screenwriter, Founder/Director of Winnipeg's Reel to Real Film Festival and Director of Mully Children's Family charitable organization in Canada.

I arranged to attend the MCF mission conference at the Mennonite Brethren Church in Winnepeg and he warmly invited me to stay in his home the coming December 2014. Dr. Mulli would fly from Kenya and address the conference where over 600 attended and a large sum was donated to Charles for children support at MCF.

I phoned the directors of MCF in Atlanta and requested materials to train me in becoming an ambassador for Florida. After sending in my commitment statements, I became the first ambassador for MCFUS non-profit. Craig Steuterman and Charley Malmquist warmly welcomed my participation to help in any way I could. They called me in mid-February 2015 and asked me to pray about having Charles Mulli speak in churches and gatherings in Sarasota during April 29 through May 3rd. I was gratified that they trusted me, but somewhat fearful of making a commitment I couldn't keep.

I would hate for Charles, Craig and Charley to come all the way here, only to have no speaking engagements. Having been an Army chaplain moving around all my career, I had no deep roots in Sarasota. Also, Julie and I had only just started attending Siesta Key Chapel, a Presbyterian church. Its commitment to ten other Christian missions already lowered the odds of a new attending visitor introducing one more mission project to an already crowded venue and overstretched mission's budget.

How would I make any inroads for a new mission?

I didn't know anyone in town. So, I spent several evenings in prayer. God had to open doors I didn't know existed. Then, the miracles began.

My phone rang one day and a voice I hadn't heard since my high school graduation, greeted me: "Dixey, it's Tim Moran. I saw your announcement on Facebook that you've retired, and you also want to help Charles Mulli. I just wanted to let you know I'm only 20 miles from you and I've lived here for 30 years in Bradenton. If there is anything I can do to help you with the Mully Children's Family, let me know.

"I know many important key people in town, and I worked at the IMG Academy that Nick Bolletteri built to train world champion tennis Olympians: Venus and Serena Williams, Andre Agassi and Maria Sharapova to name a few. I am also president of Myco Trailers. We build boat trailers for the Marine Special Forces and for the two-million-dollar Thunder Boats which we ship around the world."

I recalled that Tim had been a mover and shaker as the 1968 Brookville High Class President. We grew up a half mile from each other on the same road, Westbrook Road, in Brookville, Ohio.

Next, I remembered in the chaplaincy that there is usually a ministerial association in every city. So, I researched the city white pages to look for a ministerial alliance. Sure enough, I found a Sarasota Ministerial Alliance (SMA) directory. Chaplain Dr. Tom Pfaff founded it 17 years before. He met monthly with over 30 pastors and 20 local government and first responder group leaders.

I called Tom, introduced myself as a 26-year Army chaplain veteran and that I'd love to attend an SMA monthly meeting. After welcoming me, he introduced me to the group luncheon of 50 city leaders and said, "Share with us what's on your heart."

The group warmly encouraged me, and God gave me an open door for sharing my son's movie trailer, titled *MULLY*. The movie would not be complete for three more years, but the trailer that Lukas and Scott Haze created, left a deep impression.

Then, another Godsend—Bob Kuck, whom I'd only just met on my boat-dock, chaired the Missions and Evangelism Committee at Siesta Key Chapel. He introduced me to Rev. Art Hallett, the founder of Evangelism Explosion Prison Ministry, (EEPM). Art had established his ministry in 38 states in over 300 prisons. I began attending his ministry in local prisons. He also said he would gladly help me in any way I needed. Within two short weeks, I had connections and relationships with men and women all over Sarasota. Old friendships and new were bringing it all together. God was moving and I could barely keep in step; my fears of failure disintegrated.

Then another venture occurred simultaneously. I had gifted the book *Father to the Fatherless* to Tom Bragg of YWAMpublishing.com when I was in Dallas at a CFGC conference where I'd been asked to speak. Tom and Terri Bragg were good friends of ours since we lived in the YWAM Hurlach castle in Germany back in 1978 through 1980. Tom Bragg and Warren Walsh founded YWAM Publishing in Edmonds, Washington State (near Seattle), after leaving the castle.

Tom had become so excited about Mulli's story that he asked if I could get his authors, Janet and Geoff Benge, permission to write Charles' life story targeted for a younger audience to make it more interesting to them. Tom wanted it to become part of their series called *Christian Heroes, Then and Now.*

Julie and I knew the Benge's books. We'd read some 25 of them and listened to their audio books while traveling in our car with our grandchildren. What a divine synergy this would be on top of Charles, Craig and Charley's speaking visit. (We were later blessed to hear that Charles' wife, Esther Mulli, would be coming with him.)

I told Tom, I would check with Charles and with the U.S. non-profit leaders to get their permission. I didn't want to compete with the sales of Paul Boge's book. So, I prayed and wrote a three-page fact sheet letter to Charles extolling the benefits of such a book marketed to a teen market that already had an established audience from the Benge's previous 42 Christian Heroes book series. Today, there are 50 amazing and courageous stories of Christian missionaries of the past and present. Besides the English version, the Spanish version and audiobook CDs would expand awareness of Charles' ventures of believing God for the impossible to a greater global audience.

When Charles approved the YWAM Christian Heroes series publishing of his story, Tom wanted to tell the Benges, but Janet was busy writing a book in the Andes Mountains of Peru and out of contact. She was in for a big surprise. When wrapping up her book interview with Dr. Klaus Dieter John on building a 2.5-million-dollar hospital by faith in Cura Hausa, Peru, she posed a final question to Klaus:

"If you were not working here building this hospital to give free medical care to the indigenous Peruvian Indians, what would you be doing?" Klaus answered, "I would be working with Dr. Charles Mulli in Ndalani, Kenya; he is the mentor for all that I do. You need to write your next book on his life! Have you ever heard of him?"

"No, this is the first time I have heard his name," Janet responded, "I'll have to check him out when I get back home to Orlando."

The next time Tom Bragg called, he told me that Janet asked him if he knew anyone who knew Charles Mulli. Tom told her that my son's movie on Mulli's life was in postproduction and that the Mulli's would be coming to Sarasota in four weeks, April 29th. We set four days for the Benges to interview Charles and Esther in my condo. God even provided a neighbor who donated his empty condo to them for their stay (the Benges lived three hours away).

Since we'd never met the Benges, our MCF itinerary became a double blessing. Janet had time to give me writing guidelines to follow and began encouraging me to write my own life's story. To think that I might one day become an author was a stretch too far for even my imagination. But, sitting in and overhearing the interviews of the Benges with the Mullis for a new book triggered the thought *Maybe I could write a book someday.*

God causes multiple synergies to coincide when you move in faith. Our entire time together was blessed by our speaking engagement at IMG Academy arranged by my colleagues, Tim Moran and Chaplain Butch Morley, leader of John 3:16 Ministries at the IMG Academy chapel.

Having the Mullis, the Benges, Craig, Charley and Tim Moran in our home was one of the greatest joys and privileges in our lives. The collaborative efforts of such visionaries were explosive.

42

Riding on the "Stroke" Rollercoaster

TWO YEARS LATER, AT AGE 67, I encountered the most difficult time of my life. Probably because it shook three areas of my life at their deepest foundations: control, independence and mortality. I will begin with a metaphor. A roller coaster called *stroke* can appear out of nowhere. When its door opens for you, it doesn't ask your name, your sex, your age, your race, your social status, your education or career. It begins without warning and refusal to get on is not an option. The "Stroke" roller coaster appeared for me and still wields its power over my life. I share the following information to help others should they face a similar situation.

One prodigious day, November 17, 2017, Julie and I drove from Sarasota across the state to Boynton Beach to premier the *MULLY* movie to an audience. As an Army chaplain with 30 years of active duty, I had addressed crowds many hundreds of times. That night was no different. After Walter Hagen, my host, introduced me at his church, on his cue I stood up in front of a group of 70 people.

For five minutes, I introduced *MULLY* – the movie. I felt that sharing the movie with other church groups would deeply touch and impress others as it had moved me. I wanted to help increase the number of sponsors for supporting orphans. My recent retirement provided me the support, time and opportunity to do this.

After the opening words, I walked back to my seat and sat down with Julie in the front row for this first screening in Florida. The lights dimmed and the movie began.

Something deep within me altered my attention from the movie. A disturbing physical sensation alerted me that something was amiss. I wondered *did I slur my words when speaking*? I looked at Julie; she didn't act as if she noticed anything wrong with me. Then, without warning, my right arm felt heavy, almost as if I held a 20 lb. dumbbell. It was hard to lift my arm without help from my left hand. *What's going on*?

The familiar score of the music from the London Philharmonic orchestrated by composer Benjamin Wallfisch, filled the room as the scene from the Kibera slum district in Nairobi, Kenya came into view. All eyes were on that incredible sight. Just seconds later, I noticed my right leg was also getting heavy, feeling like a 40 lb. weight.

Deeply concerned, I leaned over and whispered to Julie that I needed to step outside and check something. "I am just not feeling right." I still could not fathom the scope and seriousness of my situation, and the audience didn't notice my stepping out to the side in the dark making my way toward the back. As my right arm dangled and numbed, my gait staggered. *What the heck is this?* I struggled for an answer.

Am I having a heart attack?

Strangely, I felt no pain. I got Jill's attention (our hostess, Walt's wife), and motioned her outside. "Something is wrong with me. How far is the ER?"

"Five minutes."

"Could you take me now?"

I asked Jill to inform Julie that I was feeling strange and wanted to get a doctor's opinion at the ER, and would she ask Julie to close the program and come join me after the movie. Little did I know that I'd stepped onto a rollercoaster called 'stroke.'

At the ER, I jumped out and limped into the check-in. Jill parked the car and followed me so she could tell Julie my diagnosis. With no one in line, I explained the symptoms to the receptionist. "I think I'm having a heart attack, but I don't feel any pain." She countered "You're having a stroke, sit down and fill out these forms."

That's not what I wanted to hear; I wanted doctors now, ASAP. The forms were for phone, insurance, identification, address, next of kin and medical history. I filled them out and turned them in. My right hand could still write at the time. She said a doctor would see me shortly.

Within minutes, about five doctors rushed in and escorted me into an ER cubicle for questioning and said I'd need to get an MRI right away. This was more of what I hoped would happen! You could see they'd done this drill before; it gave me some sense of comfort. They confirmed I was in the midst of a stroke. My blood pressure was 208/110. It's strange I had no physical sensation with my blood pressure being so high. *Is that why they call stroke the 'silent killer'?* They whisked my gurney down the corridor, into an elevator, and toward the MRI room. (I was familiar with many MRIs I had taken while in the Army.) Within 25 minutes they had the results and wheeled me back to the ER ward. A group of eight medical specialists discussed the data.

Julie then walked in and immediately did a double take at the sight of the IV tubes and monitors hooked up to me and the crowd of doctors. Tears began streaming down her face; I felt badly for her as she leaned over me.

From the MRI they explained to her the ischemic (blood clot) stroke in my brain's left basal ganglia and suggested only one treatment of choice to try to dissolve it, a clot-busting medication called tPA, tissue plasminogen activator. This medication is given only within four hours of symptom onset and can possibly dissolve (bust) the clot. The faster you get it, the higher the odds of recovery … but there's a catch.

The tPA causes brain bleeding and brings death in 6 out of every 100 stroke patients who receive it. Of those who elect to take it, it boosts chances for significant stroke recovery from 40% to 70% improving the odds. But that's not perfect. If the tPA had no effect, the stroke could still cause death, hemiparesis or hemiplegia in the remaining 30% of patients. I only understood the first symptom … death.

I cannot describe to you the complex decision of facing the onset of paralysis and possible death. Only two hours before, I felt in perfect health. One minute I'm fine; the next I'm facing death. Spasticity began settling into my right foot, ankle, hand and shoulder. With the ongoing stroke I could only hope that my brain had full mental cognition as we made the decision. Should I be the one even making this decision? Could I assess my situation fully and objectively and under the pressure of time?

I looked helplessly at Julie. Her eyes reflected the terror besieging her heart. We were supposed to be driving back home tomorrow.

"Dixey, I don't want you to die! This is crazy – it's a nightmare – this can't be happening to us!" Silently, I cried *Where are you, God?*

The doctors were quite insistent that we decide expeditiously. We were already over two hours into this and four hours was the maximum period allowed for injecting the tPA after stroke onset. Julie and I prayed together and asked God for guidance, healing and peace. I gave the doctors a thumbs-up to start the tPA injection.

The odds were in my favor with the tPA. The head doctor brought the Medical Liability Release contract for me to sign and lost no time starting the IV. I did not know at the time that: *'Of the 750,000 stroke victims in the USA occurring each year, the silent killer takes 150,000. That's about a one in five ratio."* Death makes no deals.

The tPA IV drip lasted an hour. They repeated my gurney trip for another MRI afterward and returned me to the ER ward where the doctors walked in with the new MRI results in their hands. Our hearts sank when we saw their faces. "We are sorry to inform you that the post tPA MRI reveals that the clot remains, it did not dissolve."

The MRI revealed a white spot about the size of a golf ball in the middle of the grey matter of my left basal ganglia. The clot buster miracle drug had failed its mission.

I couldn't walk out as signs of the stroke began appearing with restricted hand, arm and leg movement. I was told, "They will take you to the Heart

Intensive Care Unit, as our Brain ICU is full. There you will have a 24-hour ICU nurse who will make you as comfortable as possible and monitor your life support. Sorry, there is nothing more we can do. The debilitating stroke effects may stop soon or continue for days. Every stroke is different. Julie can sleep in the ICU if she likes." *Would I die?*

Four days later, I awoke to the worst realization in my life.

My entire right side was paralyzed! My right arm didn't move; my right leg wouldn't move; my toes and fingers wouldn't move. The pain from the spasticity swelling made it feel like they were squeezed in a vise. The whole right side of my face was frozen in place. I couldn't move my right eye, or the right side of my tongue or lip.

I tried to speak, only getting out six long slurred words in one minute. The right half of my vocal cords and epiglottis froze in place. My voice was distorted; no one could understand me except the ICU nurse. My right lip muscles had lost their tone.

The corner of my lip drooped down over half an inch. I tried turning over in my bed with my left side which worked perfectly … but I couldn't. My entire right side was dead. I could not move without both sides working properly.

This ischemic stroke had taken its toll. *Is this to be the story of the rest of my life?* What grand purpose of God could come from this? And what about Julie? I couldn't imagine her pain and fear. Would she want to live with an invalid, possibly not having the emotional, mental and physical strength to deal with this?

Feeling utterly confused and abandoned, I gave up trying to figure it all out, falling back to sleep, exhausted and terrified.

43

Stroke Recovery

EIGHT MORE DAYS PASSED. An orderly pushed me in a wheelchair from my bed to the curbside. Aids lifted my helpless body (with right-sided hemiplegia – a severe or complete loss of strength or paralysis on one side of the body) into the front seat of our SUV. Julie drove me from the east coast hospital to Sarasota for the arranged stroke recovery therapy.

The contrast between the old hospital wing I left to the new $55 million Sarasota rehab pavilion stole my breath. It's hard to imagine that someone designed, planned, funded, built and staffed an entire center just for folks like me with strokes who would come here in the future. Just having the positive attitude of the employees, therapists and my fellow stroke survivors around me, encouraged me to work as hard as I could at recovery therapy exercises. They told me I could possibly walk again! That statement was really hard to believe, since I had no control over any part of my right side, not even my pinky.

When God hadn't healed me instantly as He had done when I prayed for others earlier in my ministry, I realized it would be an inch-by-inch fight to get my life back.

Every day felt like climbing Mt. Everest. The smallest move demanded my utmost exertion.

The greatest experience in my next 30 days at the Stroke Rehabilitation Pavilion occurred on day 23. Therapists had spent two weeks with me using a vector. It's a marvelous device which holds you in a body harness with cables dangling from the ceiling on a monorail track. It walks you down the hallway teaching balance, coordination and control. Looking like Pinocchio, dangling from cables, I learned to walk again. I covered a distance of 40 feet using a cane; then I collapsed from exhaustion. I slowly limped a few steps more with my cane each day. What would I do with my life now?

I struggled over the next two years to get over my anger with God for letting this happen to me. No magical cures were found, nor instant healing or tricks. Nothing resolved the grief, pain and disappointment. I shuddered to think what would happen if a second stroke occurred when I learned that 50% of stroke victims have a second stroke within a year. Death stared at me. Fear sometimes overwhelmed me.

Since I still had the power of choice, I decided to begin speaking in churches again to help raise support for orphans. I would use humor as much as possible. My muddled and desperately slowed and slurred speech certainly tested the patience and kindness of congregations; yet they encouraged me in my setback, urging me to trust God. I still struggled with everything in life—even God.

Earlier, I shared about how God brought the Benges together with the Mulli's to create the book, *Charles Mulli, We Are Family*. Now, God challenged me to a new venture of faith—to begin writing a Mully Movie Study Guide (MMSG) to help integrate Mulli's faith principles into life. My son, Lukas helped me immensely with graphic design artists and getting funding for publishing, marketing and shipping.

My friend, Rev. Art Hallett, encouraged me to write the study guide to help change prisoners' self-esteem when they became Christians after viewing the rags to riches story of Charles Mulli's life. Combining the *MULLY* movie with the MMSG booklet as an eight-week study course, led to the conversions of over 70 prisoners, both men and women in two nearby prisons. Then, through my denomination, CFGC, 10 prison chaplains helped me to get the MMSG course into over 250 prisons in eight states.

Focusing on the needs of others incentivized me to begin writing my life's story once again. God intervened to encourage me with a return visit by Charles Mulli in March 2019, two years after my stroke. This time, Rev. Art Hallett and Gina Burns of EEPM sponsored Mulli's round-trip and most of the speaking engagements.

We planned 14 speaking venues in nine days. I will share three of those events which had monumental impact.

44

The Promised Doubling

PUTTING TOGETHER A SPEAKING schedule for an extremely busy and industrious person is a joy to undertake. Organizing events for visiting VIPs throughout my career in the Army made this activity second nature. Art and Gina scheduled his main church events, their EEPM annual fundraiser dinner highlighted by two prison visitations where Charles would share directly with prisoners who had taken my MMSG course.

Charles had planned to speak at the 2018 EEPM banquet the previous year but had to cancel due of the severe draught in Kenya keeping him in-country. We were thrilled when Charles wrote to say he could make the 2019 Prison Ministry fund-raiser banquet.

On day four of his nine-day schedule, a new event popped up totally off our radar. It became the largest event: a 60-nation satellite broadcast of the *MULLY* Movie Short Documentary (40 minutes) and a Q & A interview with Charles on TV at Trinity Broadcasting Network Studio in Dallas. God helped us rearrange our tightly packed schedule so as not to lose one venue.

Working with Art, Gina and Charles has been one of the greatest honors in my life. To watch God, fill in the nine days from a blank slate to an overpacked speaking schedule is both fulfilling and scary. Could God make the time schedule flow without overlap and conflict? As I watched Dr. Mulli glide through these constant changes and challenges with grace, I learned quite a bit about patience and trust.

Nothing ever rattled him! "God will take care of it," he'd always say.

* * *

I have heard of asking God for a specific goal but had only implemented such a strategy twice in my life. Once, when Julie and I trusted God to release $1,000 for the Anastasis ship purchase in 1978 which came in within the next four months.

Secondly, when (Skip) James Taylor and I invited Billy Graham's son, Franklin Graham to our Wilmore Presbyterian Church missions conference, back in 1984 while in seminary. We trusted God for an annual $8,000 mission's *faith pledge* goal. God exceeded our goal! By the end of the year over $11,000 came in. Could I trust God for a certain number of orphan sponsors from Charles' coming visit? I certainly didn't want to see Charles come and go with no sponsorship pledges as happened on his last visit. I learned from Dr. Mulli that planting a seed and growing the harvest takes time.

The *MULLY* movie my son produced had played in over 1,000 theaters throughout the U.S. and Canada in October and November 2017. In January 2019, I called up the www.MCFUS.org sponsorship department and asked, "How many sponsors for MCF orphans are in Florida?" When I heard that there were nine Florida families sponsoring children, I prayed and asked the Lord, *Should I pray that You will give us another nine orphan sponsors, Lord?* I waited and prayed for several days.

About the fifth day, the Lord spoke to me in almost what sounded like an audible voice. "*No, Dixey, do not pray for nine sponsors. I want you to pray that I will double the number of Florida sponsors by 18 more!*"

Did I hear God correctly? *You mean You want me to pray for 18 more new orphan sponsors?* That doubled-nine number exceeded anything I thought or could believe for, but I decided to believe God for it. I prayed a great deal, and at each church challenged the congregations to become part of the 18 sponsors who would pledge $50 a month. I asked them to come to the back table and sign up after Dr. Mulli spoke.

I would say, "Perhaps some of you are to be part of that answer." A few people came and pledged support at each church. By the final day at the last church, Dr. Mulli had to leave early to catch his flight back to Kenya before the service ended.

Still, I needed four more orphan sponsors. I stood in back as people responded to the challenge. When the fourth person signed their name and made their pledge, I let out with "Alleluia, glory to God." We all rejoiced!

But two weeks later, when I checked on all those who followed through, I found only fourteen had sent in their first month's support.

Lord, I cannot call them and remind them, this is a faith pledge between them and You. Will you help us get the remaining four children covered somehow?

Meantime, I joined the Sarasota Southside Rotary Club in May that I had visited over the previous four years. Six months later, Dale Vollrath, funding director, told me the Rotary Board had decided to sponsor four orphans for the next year and sent me a $2,400 check for MCF that week! God answered our *doubling goal* prayer to sponsor the eighteen new orphans! Once again, God responded in a remarkable unexpected way.

* * *

Following the voice that spoke to me as a high school senior led me on this journey with the divine to experience a life marked by miracles.

Afterword

WITHIN A YEAR FOLLOWING my massive stroke, after hundreds of hours of physical and occupational therapy, I put the wheelchair into the closet and began always walking with a cane. I also earned back my driving privileges. Getting my license at 68 felt greater than it did the first time when I was 16. With my newfound freedom and independence restored, my life returned closer to normal.

Because of the stroke, I set aside writing this book which I'd worked on for the previous three years. With my dominant right hand still totally useless at typing, I'd had to learn typing all over again, only using my left hand. My typing rate used to be 70 wpm with both hands. Now, with hundreds of hours of practice, my left hand alone is up to 25 wpm. Doctors and therapists cheered my recovery every time I had checkups.

Life is still thrilling and quite busy. One of the greatest lessons I have learned from my stroke is: *I am not my body.* I am just borrowing it for a while. My body's limitations do not define me, nor do they limit my God or what He can do through me. I will cast off this body someday, but until then, I'll keep moving; trusting Him for greater things.

My stroke severely changed my life and Julie's. But life's changes bring new creative forces to merge in ways that drive us forward. We now support five Mully children and pray that we can expand that number. Please pray about joining me and supporting a child through www.mcfus.org or if God places the www.mercyships.org ministry or www.eeprisonministry.com on your heart, know that they are certified by the highest ethical and accounting standards of Charitable organizations.

I trust that God has used these stories to open your eyes to His manifold wisdom, His personal presence and purpose in your own life and His boundless love.

Until the next time when we meet in person or on print my friends, know that you can become the miracle that someone is praying for.

Acknowledgements

Marked by Miracles came to exist through the encouragement, support and contributions of many people over the last seven years. I want to thank:

* Julie, my wife for constant encouragement and prayers.
* Lukas, my son for his excellent tech support, assistance and editing.
* David Boyd, former YWAM Hurlach Director and Evangelist Dr. Charles Mulli, founder of Mully Children's Family-Kenya for their inspiring Forewords.
* My editors, Janet Benge and Sonia Naea.
* M. Sue Alexander of Suxander Publishing for her editing and formatting expertise, friendship, constant encouragement and guidance. Sue came up with the name for this book, *Marked by Miracles*, for which I am very grateful.
* Joyce Keller, for her editing assistance, hospitality and prayers.
* My first readers: my brother, Rev. Dr. Bruce Behnken, Director of Go to Nations, Manilla, Philippines; Chaplain (Colonel-Ret.) James A. Agnew; Rev. Skip Taylor; Lars Walker, Author; Dwight Coleman and Kent Ernsting.
* All of those who read my book and wrote reviews: Rev. Dr. Maxie Dunnam; Donald Stephens, Founder of Mercy Ships; Lieutenant General Robert B. Flowers, former Director of Army Corps of Engineers; Chaplain (Rear Admiral) Brent W. Scott, U. S. Navy; Jim Orred, Ambassador-at-Large, Youth With a Mission (YWAM); Rev. Dr. James (Skip) W. Taylor, Jr., Walk thru the Bible Seminars; Keith and Marion Warrington, Co-Directors, YWAM, Berlin; Dwight Coleman, Consultant, Project Manager; Paul H. Boge, Author of Father to the Fatherless and Director of Mully Children's Family, Canada; Dr. David Chotka; Dr Klon Kitchen, CFGC.
* My lifetime mentors: Chaplain (Colonel-Ret.) James Agnew, and Chaplain (Lieutenant Colonel-Ret.) Richard Thompson.
* My 'Get Published Now' coaching team: Tamra Reichardt and Cristina Smith.
* Last, but definitely not least, Chaplain (Colonel-Ret.) E. H. Jim Ammerman, U.S. Army, Founder of Chaplaincy, Full Gospel Churches (CFGC), my ecclesiastical endorser, mentor and friend from 1985 thru 2012, and his lovely wife, Charlene Ammerman, co-founder of CFGC.

End Notes

You can read some of the 40-year history beginning with the M/V Anastasis Ship in Don Stephens' book, *Ships of Mercy,* and catch up on current operations on www.mercyships.org website. Don's book, *Trial By Trial,* tells some of the growing pains that occurred while preparing the Anastasis ship for the humanitarian refit in Greece. The *Anastasis* launched some two years later for humanitarian ministry throughout Africa and the Mercy Ships continues today. With over 25,000 volunteers over the next 29 years, Don's vision helped hundreds of thousands receive healing and medical operations. Don just recently designed, built and outfitted a new humanitarian ship to add to the fleet called the *Global Mercy.*

See the Free Movie – MULLY at www.mcfus.org

MULLY the true story of Charles Mully, whose unlikely stratospheric rise to wealth and power leaves him questioning his own existence, searching for meaning in life. Against the better judgment of family and community, ***MULLY*** sets out to enrich the fate of orphaned children across Kenya. Jeopardizing his own life and the security of his family, Charles Mully risks everything and sets in motion a series of events that is nothing short of astonishing. Charles has created the World's Largest Family that has grown to over 4,000 today.

Evangelism Explosion Prison Ministry

Rev. Arthur Hallett is a man of many talents. He is both an accomplished and talented musician and songwriter. Arthur has completed several CD's. A concert flautist, Arthur leads praise and worship, preaches and teaches as an evangelist in prisons and churches across the country. However, Arthur's life and passion are prison ministry. He ministers in 41 states to 500 prisons and 22 other nations. See his website at: www.eeprisonministry.com. Hebrews 13:3 (NIV) "Remember those in prison..."

Janet and Geoff Benge

Janet and Jeff have written 50 books for the *Christian Heroes: Then and Now Series* and 30 books for the *Heroes of History Series.* They taught writing at University of the Nations for years. If you read their books, you'll want to read them all. I highly recommend them! Check them out at: www.ywampublishing.com.

Bibliography

(Suggested for your reading Enjoyment)

Andrew, Brother (2015). *God's Smuggler,* Chosen Books

Behnken, Dixey (2017). *Mully Movie Study Guide*, Royal Palm Press

(see: www.mcfus.org, to view free movie), "MULLY"

Benge, Janet and Geoff (2014). Christian Heroes, Then and Now: *Klaus-Dieter John, "Hope in the Land of the Incas"*, YWAM Publishing.

Benge, Janet and Geoff (2017). Christian Heroes, Then and Now: *Charles Mulli, "We Are Family"*, YWAM Publishing.

Boge, Paul (2006). *Father to the Fatherless*, Bayridge Books

Boge, Paul (2012). *Hope for the Hopeless*, Castle Quay Books

Bubeck, Mark (1975). *The Adversary,* Moody Publishing

Cunningham, Loren (2001). *Is That Really You, God?,* YWAM Publishing

Dawson, Joy (1991). *Some of the Ways of God in Healing,* YWAM Publishing

Dawson, Joy (1997). *Intercession, Thrilling and Fulfilling,* YWAM Publishing

(see: PrinciplesforEffectiveIntercession-JoyDawson)

Grubb, Norman (2017). *Rees Howells, Intercessor,* CLC Publications.

Stephens, Don (2005). *Ships of Mercy,* Thomas Nelson, Inc.

(see: www.mercyships.org for the most updated information)

Stephens, Don (1985). *Trial by Trial,* Harvest House Publishers

Richardson, Don (1981). *Eternity in Their Hearts*, Bethany House

Richardson, Don (2005). *Peace Child*, Bethany House Publisher

Permissions and Credits

Front Cover Enhancement by Adam Wheeler

Front Cover Photo Permission by Julianne Behnken

Cover Design by Christine Roszak

Back Cover Photo Permission by Kay Yoder

Back Cover Photo of Sunset: Istock by Getty Images

MMSG Photo Permission by Lukas Behnken

Could you please help me improve? Please excuse any error you find and notify me at my email so that I may correct it. Thank You!

Study Guide by CH Dixey R. Behnken

MULLY MOVIE STUDY GUIDE
Seven Themes of Change in Mulli's Life – Reflection & Application

Study 1 – Values, Beliefs and Change
Study 2 – Forgiveness
Study 3 – From Abandonment to Saving the Abandoned
Study 4 – Rejection, Bitterness, Suicide
Study 5 – The Power of One
Study 6 – Choosing Faith
Study 7 – Sowing and Reaping

Contact: dixeybehnkenbooks@gmail.com to purchase, sold at cost + postage

CHRISTIAN HEROES: THEN & NOW
Charles Mulli: We Are Family
Janet & Geoff Benge

Purchase at: www.YWAMpublishing.com

Author's Special Book Offer
On Marked by Miracles

for:

Conferences and Volume purchases

Please contact: dixeybehnkenbooks@gmail.com

or:

Also available for Speaking engagements,
Interviews and Missions Conferences

Please contact: dixeybehnkenbooks@gmail.com

PLEASE VISIT MY WEBSITE:

www.markedbymiracles.com

THE UNITED STATES OF AMERICA

TO ALL WHO SHALL SEE THESE PRESENTS, GREETING: THIS IS TO CERTIFY THAT THE PRESIDENT OF THE UNITED STATES OF AMERICA AUTHORIZED BY ACT OF CONGRESS 20 JULY 1942 HAS AWARDED

THE LEGION OF MERIT

TO LIEUTENANT COLONEL DIXEY R. BEHNKEN, CHAPLAIN, UNITED STATES ARMY

FOR EXCEPTIONALLY MERITORIOUS SERVICE, UPON RETIREMENT, WHILE SERVING IN NUMEROUS POSITIONS OF GREAT RESPONSIBILITY THROUGHOUT A CAREER SPANNING 26 YEARS OF MILITARY SERVICE, CULMINATING AS THE BRIGADE CHAPLAIN, 22ND SIGNAL BRIGADE, 5TH SIGNAL COMMAND, UNITED STATES ARMY, EUROPE, AND SEVENTH ARMY. HIS SUSTAINED SUPERIOR PERFORMANCE, SELFLESS SERVICE, AND COMPASSIONATE MENTORSHIP DIRECTLY CONTRIBUTED TO THE SUCCESS OF NUMEROUS UNITS THROUGHOUT HIS CAREER. HIS DEDICATION TO DUTY AND SINCERE CONCERN FOR SOLDIERS WERE IN KEEPING WITH THE HIGHEST TRADITIONS OF MILITARY SERVICE AND SET A STANDARD FOR ALL TO EMULATE. HIS OUTSTANDING LEADERSHIP AND CONTINUOUS SUPPORT OF THE GLOBAL WAR ON TERRORISM REFLECT GREAT CREDIT UPON HIM, HIS UNIT, AND THE UNITED STATES ARMY.

BY ORDER OF THE SECRETARY OF THE ARMY

THIS 1ST DAY OF SEPTEMBER 2007

PERMANENT ORDERS 136-7
16 MAY 2007
Headquarters,
United States Army, Europe,
and Seventh Army

GARY D. SPEER
Lieutenant General, U.S. Army
Deputy Commanding General

Previous edition is obsolete

Manufactured by Amazon.ca
Bolton, ON

24551685R00085